BEHOLD THE MAN

BEHOLD THE MAN

A Biblical Narrative of the Last Days of Jesus Christ

MICHAEL JAMES FITZGERALD

Overdue Books

Scriptural content from the King James Version of the New Testament.

Second Print Edition, January 25, 2014 (rev. 20191124)

ISBN-13: 978-1-887309-28-8

ISBN-10: 1-887309-28-4

Cover art *Jesus Said to Her, "Mary,"* by William Whitaker © By Intellectual Reserve, Inc. Used by permission.

Overdue Books
http://www.overduebooks.com

To Cristi

INTRODUCTION

This book is the fruit of a study I began during the Easter season of 1986. It was then that I began an earnest study in the New Testament of the events surrounding the last week of the mortal life of Jesus Christ.

I began then to put together in my own mind the enormous puzzle of the accounts of the Passion of Christ as told in the gospel accounts of the New Testament. The gospels of Matthew, Mark, Luke and John each provide unique details about the events leading to Jesus' death. My goal in writing this book was to: (1) identify the unique details from each of the gospels relating to the Passion; (2) to unify those details; and (3) to present them in an easy-to-read, narrative format.

The source for this book is the King James Version of the Bible. While the book is completely based on scripture, I have updated punctuation and paragraphing, altered some capitalization and pronouns, and added single and double quotation marks as appropriate. I have also added conjunctive or transitional words (without setting them off with brackets) and have deleted some words to help the flow of the narrative.

The Passion of Jesus Christ is the greatest tragedy and triumph in history. I have never found anything to compare with it. I have faith and a sure witness that Jesus was more than a man, that He is the Only Begotten Son of God, the Savior of the world.

Though I have made every effort to avoid them, any errors or omissions that have crept into this book are solely my responsibility. I have done the best I could to be as true to the original gospels as I possibly could and to combine the material into a reasonable, logical storyline. Ultimately, these interpretations may change over time as my understanding deepens. Regardless of misgivings, if any reader is touched by this miraculous story, it will have been worth the effort.

❈ I ❈

PROLOGUE

THE SON OF MAN SHALL BE BETRAYED

And Jesus went before them, and they were apart in the way, going up to Jerusalem, and as they followed, they were amazed and afraid.

Then he took unto him again the twelve disciples, and began to tell them what things should happen unto him, saying, "Behold, we go up to Jerusalem, and all things that are written by the prophets concerning the Son of man shall be accomplished.

"And the Son of man shall be betrayed and delivered up unto the chief priests, and unto the scribes, and they shall condemn him to death, and shall deliver him to the Gentiles. And they shall mock him, and shall scourge him, and shall spit upon him, and he shall be spitefully entreated.

"And they shall put him to death, and the third day, he shall rise again."

And they understood none of these things, and this saying was hid from them, neither knew they the things which were spoken.

Matt. 20:17–19; Mark 10:32–34; Luke 18:31–34

AN ALABASTER BOX OF VERY PRECIOUS OINTMENT

Then Jesus, six days before the passover, was in Bethany, in the house of Simon the leper, where Lazarus was which had been dead, whom he had raised from the dead.

There they made him a supper, and Martha served, but Lazarus was one of them that sat at the table with him.

Then came unto him Mary having an alabaster box of very precious ointment of spikenard, very costly; and she brake the box, and poured it on his head, as he sat at meat. And anointed the feet of Jesus, and wiped his feet with her hair, and the house was filled with the odour of the ointment.

And there were some of his disciples that saw it and had indignation within themselves, and they murmured against her.

Then saith one of his disciples, Judas Iscariot, Simon's son, which should betray him, "To what purpose is this waste of the ointment made? For this might have been sold for more than three hundred pence and given to the poor."

This he said, not that he cared for the poor; but because he was a thief, and had the bag, and bare what was put therein.

When Jesus understood it, he said unto them, "Let her alone. Why trouble ye the woman, for she hath wrought a good work upon me. For ye have the poor with you always, and whensoever ye will, ye may do them good. But me ye have not always.

"For she hath done what she could: She is come aforehand to anoint my body for my burial.

"Verily I say unto you, wheresoever this gospel shall be preached throughout the whole world, this also that she hath done shall be spoken of for a memorial of her."

Matt. 26:6–12; Mark 14:3–9; John 12:1–8

❧ II ❧
THE FIRST DAY OF
THE WEEK

Sunday

HOSANNA TO THE SON OF DAVID

AND IT CAME TO PASS, when they came nigh to Jerusalem, and were come unto Bethphage and Bethany, unto the mount called the mount of Olives, then sent Jesus forth two of his disciples, and saith unto them, "Go your way into the village over against you, and as soon as ye be entered into it, ye shall find an ass tied, and a colt with her, whereon yet never man sat: loose them, and bring them unto me.

"And if any man ask you, 'Why do ye loose him?' thus shall ye say unto him, 'Because the Lord hath need of him.' And straightway he will send them."

And the disciples went their way, and did as Jesus commanded them, and found even as he had said unto them—the colt tied by the door without in a place where two ways met. And they loose him.

And as they were loosing the colt, the owners thereof that stood there said unto them, "What do ye, loosing the colt?"

And they said unto them, "The Lord hath need of him," even as Jesus had commanded. And they let them go.

And they brought the ass, and the colt, to Jesus, and they cast upon the colt their garments, and they set Jesus thereon.

All this was done that it might be fulfilled which was spoken by the prophet, saying, "Tell ye the daughter of Sion, Behold, thy King cometh unto thee, and sitting upon an ass, and a colt the foal of an ass."

These things understood not his disciples at the first, but when Jesus was glorified, then remembered they that these things were written of him, and that they had done these things unto him.

And a very great multitude spread their garments in the way; others cut down branches from off the trees, and strawed them in the way.

The people therefore that was with him when he called Lazarus out of his grave, and raised him from the dead, bare record. For this cause the people also met him, for that they heard that he had done this miracle.

And when he was come nigh, even now at the descent of the mount of Olives, the whole multitude of the disciples began to rejoice and praise God with a loud voice for all the mighty works that they had seen. And the multitudes that went before, and they that followed, cried, saying, "Hosanna to the Son of David! Blessed is the King that cometh in the name of the Lord.

"Blessed be the kingdom of our father David, that cometh in the name of the Lord. Peace in heaven, and hosanna in the highest!"

And some of the Pharisees from among the multitude said unto him, "Master, rebuke thy disciples."

And he answered and said unto them, "I tell you that, if these should hold their peace, the stones would immediately cry out."

The Pharisees therefore said among themselves, "Perceive ye how ye prevail nothing? behold, the world is gone after him."

Matt. 21:10–11. 17; Mark 11:11; Luke 19:41–44

HE BEHELD THE CITY AND WEPT

And when he was come near, he beheld the city, and wept over it, saying, "If thou hadst known, even thou, at least in this thy day, the things which belong unto thy peace! But now they are hid from thine eyes.

"For the days shall come upon thee, that thine enemies shall cast a trench about thee, and compass thee round, and keep thee in on every side, and shall lay thee even with the ground, and thy children within thee. And they shall not leave in thee one stone upon another because thou knewest not the time of thy visitation."

And when he was come into Jerusalem, all the city was moved, saying, "Who is this?" And the multitude said, "This is Jesus the prophet of Nazareth of Galilee."

And Jesus entered into Jerusalem, and into the temple. And when he had looked round about upon all things, and the eventide was come, he left them, and went out of the city into Bethany with the twelve, and he lodged there.

Matt. 21:10–11. 17; Mark 11:11; Luke 19:41–44

III

THE SECOND DAY OF
THE WEEK

Monday

LET NO FRUIT GROW ON THEE

N OW IN THE MORNING, as he returned into the city, when they were come from Bethany, he was hungry. And when he saw in the way a fig tree afar off, having leaves, he came to it, if haply he might find any thing thereon.

And when he came to it, he found nothing thereon, but leaves only, for the time of figs was not yet.

And Jesus answered and said unto it, "Let no man eat fruit of thee hereafter for ever."

And his disciples heard it, and presently the fig tree withered away.

Matt. 21:18–19; Mark 12:12–14

YE HAVE MADE IT A DEN OF THIEVES

And they come to Jerusalem. And Jesus went into the temple of God and began to cast out all them that sold therein, and them that bought in the temple, and overthrew the tables of the moneychangers, and the seats of them that sold doves, and would not suffer that any man should carry any vessel through the temple.

And he taught saying unto them, "Is it not written, 'My house shall be called of all nations the house of prayer?' But ye have made it a den of thieves."

Matt. 21:12–13; Mark 11:15–17; Luke 19:45–46

OUT OF THE MOUTH OF BABES

And the blind and the lame came to him in the temple; and he healed them.

And when the chief priests and scribes saw the wonderful things that he did, and the children crying in the temple, and saying, "Hosanna to the Son of David!" they were sore displeased, and said unto him, "Hearest thou what these say?"

And Jesus saith unto them, "Yea; have ye never read, 'Out of the mouth of babes and sucklings thou hast perfected praise?'"

And he taught daily in the temple, but the scribes and chief priests and the chief of the people heard it, and sought how they might destroy him, for they feared him, but could not find what they might do, because all the people were astonished at his doctrine and very attentive to hear him.

Matt. 21:14–16; Mark 11:18; Luke 19:47–48

❧ IV ❧
THE THIRD DAY OF
THE WEEK

Tuesday

☼ 4 ☼

THE FIG TREE WITHERED AWAY

And in the morning, as they passed by, they saw the fig tree dried up from the roots. And when Peter and the disciples, calling to remembrance, saw it, they marvelled, saying unto him, "Master, behold, how soon is the fig tree which thou cursedst withered away!"

And Jesus answered and said unto them, "Verily I say unto you, if ye have faith in God and doubt not, ye shall not only do this which is done to the fig tree, but also if ye shall say unto this mountain, 'Be thou removed, and be thou cast into the sea,' and shall not doubt in thine heart, but shall believe that those things which ye saith shall come to pass, it shall be done, and ye shall have whatsoever ye saith.

"Therefore I say unto you, what things soever ye desire that ye shall ask when ye are in prayer, believe that ye receive them, and ye shall have them.

"And when ye stand praying, forgive, if ye have ought against any, that your Father also which is in heaven may forgive you your trespasses. But if ye do not forgive, neither will your Father which is in heaven forgive your trespasses."

Matt. 21:20–22; Mark 11:20–26

WHO GAVE THEE THIS AUTHORITY?

And it came to pass, that on one of those days, when they come again to Jerusalem and into the temple, as he was walking and teaching the people, the chief priests, and the scribes, and the elders came unto him, and say unto him, "Tell us, by what authority doest thou these things and who is he that gave thee this authority to do these things?"

And Jesus answered and said unto them, "I also will ask you one question, which if ye tell me, and answer me, I in like wise will tell you by what authority I do these things.

"The baptism of John, whence was it? From heaven, or of men? Answer me."

And they reasoned with themselves, saying, "If we shall say, 'From heaven,' he will say unto us, 'Why did ye not then believe him?' But if we shall say, 'Of men,' we fear the people will stone us, for all men hold John as a prophet indeed.

And they answered and said unto Jesus, "We cannot tell."

And Jesus answering saith unto them, "Neither do I tell you by what authority I do these things."

Matt. 21:23–27; Mark 11:27–33; Luke 20:1–8

A CERTAIN MAN HAD TWO SONS

"But what think ye? A certain man had two sons; and he came to the first, and said, 'Son, go work to day in my vineyard.'

"He answered and said, 'I will not.' But afterward he repented, and went.

"And he came to the second, and said likewise. And he answered and said, 'I go, sir,' and went not.

"Whether of them twain did the will of his father?"

They say unto him, "The first." Jesus saith unto them, "Verily I say unto you, that the publicans and the harlots go into the kingdom of God before you.

"For John came unto you in the way of righteousness, and ye believed him not, but the publicans and the harlots believed him. And ye, when ye had seen it, repented not afterward, that ye might believe him."

Matt. 21:28–32

A CERTAIN MAN PLANTED A VINEYARD

Then began he to speak to the people another parable: "There was a certain householder, which planted a vineyard, and hedged it round about, and digged a place for the winepress in it, and built a tower, and let it out to husbandmen, and went into a far country for a long time.

"And at the season, when the time of the fruit drew near, he sent his servants to the husbandmen, that he might receive from the husbandmen of the fruit of the vineyard.

"And the husbandmen took his servants, and beat one, and killed another, and stoned another and sent him away empty.

And again he sent unto them another servant, more than the first, and they did unto him likewise. At him they cast stones, and they beat him, wounded him in the head also, and entreated him shamefully, and sent him away empty.

"And again he sent another, and him they killed, and many others—beating some, and killing some.

"Then said the lord of the vineyard, 'What shall I do?'

"'Last of all, having yet therefore my beloved son, I will send him also last unto them, saying, it may be they will reverence him when they see him.'

"But when the husbandmen saw the son, they reasoned among themselves, saying, "This is the heir. Come, let us kill him, and let us seize on his inheritance—and the inheritance shall be ours!"

"And they caught him, and cast him out of the vineyard, and slew him.

"When therefore the lord of the vineyard cometh, what will he do unto those husbandmen?"

They say unto him, "He will come and miserably destroy those wicked men, and will let out his vineyard unto other husbandmen, which shall render him the fruits in their seasons."

And when they heard it, they said, "God forbid."

Matt. 21:33–41; Mark 12:1–9; Luke 20:9–16

THE STONE WHICH THE BUILDERS REJECTED

And Jesus beheld them, and said, "What is this then, did ye never read in the scriptures, 'The stone which the builders rejected, the same is become the head of the corner. This is the Lord's doing, and it is marvellous in our eyes?'

"Therefore say I unto you, the kingdom of God shall be taken from you, and given to a nation bringing forth the fruits thereof.

"And whosoever shall fall on this stone shall be broken, but on whomsoever it shall fall, it will grind him to powder."

And when the chief priests and Pharisees and the scribes had heard his parables, they perceived that he had spoken the parable against them. But the same hour, when they sought to lay hands on him, they feared the multitude, because they took him for a prophet. And they left him, and went their way.

Matt. 21:42–46; Mark 12:10–12; Luke 20:17–19

A KING MADE A SUPPER FOR HIS SON

And Jesus answered and spake unto them again by parables, and said, "The kingdom of heaven is like unto a certain king, which made a marriage for his son, and sent forth his servants to call them that were bidden to the wedding. And they would not come.

"Again, he sent forth other servants, saying, 'Tell them which are bidden, "Behold, I have prepared my dinner—my oxen and my fatlings are killed, and all things are ready. Come unto the marriage."'

"But they made light of it, and went their ways, one to his farm, another to his merchandise.

"And the remnant took his servants, and entreated them spitefully, and slew them.

"But when the king heard thereof, he was wroth, and he sent forth his armies, and destroyed those murderers, and burned up their city.

"Then saith he to his servants, 'The wedding is ready, but they which were bidden were not worthy. Go ye therefore into the highways, and as many as ye shall find, bid to the marriage.'

"So those servants went out into the highways, and gathered together all as many as they found, both bad and good, and the wedding was furnished with guests.

"And when the king came in to see the guests, he saw there a man which had not on a wedding garment, and he saith unto him, 'Friend, how camest thou in hither not having a wedding garment?' And he was speechless.

"Then said the king to the servants, 'Bind him hand and foot, and take him away, and cast him into outer darkness—there shall be weeping and gnashing of teeth.'

"For many are called, but few are chosen."

Matthew 22:1–14

RENDER THEREFORE UNTO CAESAR

And they watched him, and sent forth unto him their disciples—spies—and certain of the Pharisees and of the Herodians, which should feign themselves just men, and took counsel how they might entangle him in his talk, so that they might deliver him unto the power and authority of the governor.

And when they were come, they asked him, "Master, we know

that thou art true, and teachest the way of God in truth, neither carest thou for any man, for thou regardest not the person of men.

"Tell us therefore, What thinkest thou? Is it lawful for us to give tribute unto Caesar, or not? Shall we give, or shall we not give?"

But Jesus perceived their craftiness and said unto them, "Why tempt ye me, ye hypocrites? Shew me the tribute money that I may see it."

And they brought unto him a penny. And he saith unto them, "Whose is this image and superscription?"

And they said unto him, "Caesar's."

And Jesus answering said unto them, "Render therefore unto Caesar the things which are Caesar's, and unto God the things that are God's."

And they could not take hold of his words before the people. When they had heard these words, and they marvelled at his answer, and left him, and went their way and held their peace.

Matt. 22:15–22; Mark 12:13–17; Luke 20:20–26

WHOSE WIFE SHALL SHE BE?

The same day came unto him certain of the Sadducees, which deny that there is any resurrection. And they asked him, saying, "Master, Moses wrote unto us, if any man's brother die, and leave his wife behind him, and leave no children, that his brother should marry his wife, and raise up seed unto his brother.

"Now there were therefore with us seven brethren. And the first, when he had married a wife, and died, and, having no issue, left his wife unto his brother.

"Likewise the second also took her to wife, and he died, neither left he any seed. And the third likewise took her, and in like manner the seventh had her, and left no seed, and died.

"And last of all the woman died also.

"Therefore, in the resurrection, when they shall rise, whose wife of them shall she be of the seven, for they all had her to wife?

And Jesus answering said unto them, "Ye do err, not knowing the scriptures, nor the power of God.

"The children of this world marry, and are given in marriage, but they which shall be accounted worthy to obtain that world, and the resurrection, when they shall rise from the dead, neither marry, nor are given in marriage.

"Neither can they die any more, for they are equal unto the angels of God which are in heaven, and are the children of God, being the children of the resurrection.

"But as touching the resurrection of the dead, that they rise: have ye not read that which was spoken unto you by God, in the book of Moses, how in the bush God spake unto him, saying, 'I am the God of Abraham, and the God of Isaac, and the God of Jacob?'

"For God is not the God of the dead, but the God of the living, for all live unto him. Ye therefore do greatly err."

And when the multitude heard this, they were astonished at his doctrine. Then certain of the scribes answering said, "Master, thou hast well said."

Matt. 22:23–33; Mark 12:18–27; Luke 20:27–39

THOU SHALT LOVE THE LORD THY GOD

But when the Pharisees had heard that he had put the Sadducees to silence, they were gathered together.

Then one of the scribes, which was a lawyer, came, and having heard them reasoning together, and perceiving that he had answered them well, asked him a question, tempting him, and saying, "Master, which is the first and great commandment of all in the law?"

And Jesus answered him, "The first of all the commandments is, 'Hear, O Israel; The Lord our God is one Lord: and thou shalt love the Lord thy God with all thy heart, and with all thy soul, and with all thy mind, and with all thy strength.'

"This is the first and great commandment.

"And the second is like unto it, namely this, 'Thou shalt love thy neighbor as thyself.' There is none other commandment greater than these.

"On these two commandments hang all the law and the prophets.

And the scribe said unto him, "Well, Master, thou hast said the truth, for there is one God, and there is none other but he. And to love him with all the heart, and with all the understanding, and with all the soul, and with all the strength, and to love his neighbour as himself, is more than all whole burnt offerings and sacrifices."

And when Jesus saw that he answered discreetly, he said unto him, "Thou art not far from the kingdom of God."

Matt. 22:34–40; Mark 12:28–34; Luke 20:40

WHAT THINK YE OF CHRIST?

While the Pharisees were gathered together, Jesus asked them and said, while he taught in the temple, "What think ye of Christ? Whose son is he?"

They say unto him, "The Son of David."

"How say the scribes that Christ is the Son of David?"

And he saith unto them, "How then doth David himself by the Holy Ghost in the book of Psalms, call him Lord, saying, "The Lord said unto my Lord, 'Sit thou on my right hand, till I make thine enemies thy footstool?'

"If David therefore himself calleth him Lord, whence is he then his son?"

An the common people heard him gladly.

And after that, no man was able to answer him a word, neither durst any man from that day forth ask him any more questions.

Matt. 22:41–46; Mark 12:35–37; Luke 20:41–44

WO UNTO YOU, SCRIBES AND PHARISEES

Then spake Jesus in the audience of the multitude his doctrine, and to his disciples, saying, "Beware of the scribes, and the Pharisees sit in Moses' seat. All therefore whatsoever they bid you observe, that observe and do; but do not ye after their works, for they say, and do not.

"For they bind heavy burdens and grievous to be borne, and lay them on men's shoulders; but they themselves will not move them with one of their fingers. But all their works they do for to be seen of men.

"They make broad their phylacteries, and which love to go in long clothing, enlarge the borders of their garments, and love the uppermost rooms at feasts, and the chief seats in the synagogues, and to be called of men, 'Rabbi, Rabbi' and love salutations in the marketplaces.

"But be not ye called 'Rabbi,' for one is your Master, even Christ, and all ye are brethren. And call no man your father upon the earth: for one is your Father, which is in heaven. Neither be ye called masters, for one is your Master, even Christ.

"But he that is greatest among you shall be your servant. And whosoever shall exalt himself shall be abased; and he that shall humble himself shall be exalted.

"But woe unto you, scribes and Pharisees, hypocrites! For ye shut up the kingdom of heaven against men. For ye neither go in your-selves, neither suffer ye them that are entering to go in.

"Woe unto you, scribes and Pharisees, hypocrites! Which devour widows' houses, and for a pretence make long prayers. These shall receive greater damnation.

"Woe unto you, scribes and Pharisees, hypocrites! For ye compass sea and land to make one proselyte, and when he is made, ye make him twofold more the child of hell than yourselves.

"Woe unto you, ye blind guides, which say, 'Whosoever shall swear by the temple, it is nothing, but whosoever shall swear by the gold of the temple, he is a debtor!'

"Ye fools and blind! For whether is greater, the gold, or the temple that sanctifieth the gold?

"And, 'Whosoever shall swear by the altar, it is nothing, but whosoever sweareth by the gift that is upon it, he is guilty.'

"Ye fools and blind! For whether is greater, the gift, or the altar that sanctifieth the gift?

"Whoso therefore shall swear by the altar, sweareth by it, and by all things thereon. And whoso shall swear by the temple, sweareth by it, and by him that dwelleth therein. And he that shall swear by heaven, sweareth by the throne of God, and by him that sitteth thereon.

"But woe unto you, scribes and Pharisees, hypocrites! For ye pay tithe of mint and anise and cummin and rue and all manner of herbs, and have omitted the weightier matters of the law, judgment, mercy, faith and the love of God. These ought ye to have done, and not to leave the other undone.

"Ye blind guides, which strain at a gnat, and swallow a camel.

"Woe unto you, scribes and Pharisees, hypocrites! For ye make clean the outside of the cup and of the platter, but within they are full of extortion and excess. Thou blind Pharisee, cleanse first that which is within the cup and platter, that the outside of them may be clean also.

"Woe unto you, scribes and Pharisees, hypocrites! For ye are like unto whited sepulchres, which indeed appear beautiful outward, but are within full of dead men's bones, and of all uncleanness.

"Even so ye also outwardly appear righteous unto men, but within ye are full of hypocrisy and iniquity.

"Woe unto you, scribes and Pharisees, hypocrites! Because ye build the tombs of the prophets, and garnish the sepulchres of the righteous, and say, 'If we had been in the days of our fathers, we would not have been partakers with them in the blood of the prophets.'

"Wherefore ye be witnesses unto yourselves, that ye are the children of them which killed the prophets.

"Fill ye up then the measure of your fathers.

"Ye serpents, ye generation of vipers, how can ye escape the damnation of hell?

"Wherefore, behold, I send unto you prophets, and wise men, and scribes: and some of them ye shall kill and crucify. And some of them shall ye scourge in your synagogues, and persecute them from city to city, that upon you may come all the righteous blood shed upon the earth, from the blood of righteous Abel unto the blood of Zechariah son of Barachias, whom ye slew between the temple and the altar.

"Verily I say unto you, All these things shall come upon this generation.

"O Jerusalem, Jerusalem, thou that killest the prophets, and stonest them which are sent unto thee—how often would I have gathered thy children together, even as a hen gathereth her chickens under her wings, and ye would not!

"Behold, your house is left unto you desolate. For I say unto you, ye shall not see me henceforth, till ye shall say, 'Blessed is he that cometh in the name of the Lord.'"

Matt. 23:1–39; Mark 12:38–40; Luke 20:45–47

A CERTAIN POOR WIDOW

And Jesus sat over against the treasury, and looked up, and saw the rich men casting money into the treasury. And many that were rich cast in much.

And he saw also there a certain poor widow, and she threw in thither two mites which make a farthing.

And he called unto him his disciples, and saith unto them, "Verily I say unto you, that this poor widow hath cast more in, than all they which have cast into the treasury. For all they did cast in of their abundance unto the offerings of God, but she of her want did cast in all that she had, even all her living."

Mark 12:41–44; Luke 21:1–4

EXCEPT A CORN OF WHEAT FALL

And there were certain Greeks among them that came up to worship at the feast. The same came therefore to Philip, which was of Bethsaida of Galilee, and desired him, saying, "Sir, we would see Jesus."

Philip cometh and telleth Andrew, and again Andrew and Philip tell Jesus.

And Jesus answered them, saying, "The hour is come, that the Son of man should be glorified. Verily, verily, I say unto you, except a corn of wheat fall into the ground and die, it abideth alone, but if it die, it bringeth forth much fruit.

"He that loveth his life shall lose it, and he that hateth his life in this world shall keep it unto life eternal.

"If any man serve me, let him follow me, and where I am, there shall also my servant be. If any man serve me, him will my Father honour.

"Now is my soul troubled, and what shall I say? 'Father, save me from this hour'? But for this cause came I unto this hour.

"Father, glorify thy name."

Then came there a voice from heaven, saying, "I have both glorified it, and will glorify it again."

The people therefore, that stood by, and heard it, said that it thundered. Others said, "An angel spake to him."

Jesus answered and said, "This voice came not because of me, but for your sakes. Now is the judgment of this world. Now shall the prince of this world be cast out.

"And I, if I be lifted up from the earth, will draw all men unto me."

This he said, signifying what death he should die.

The people answered him, "We have heard out of the law that Christ abideth for ever, and how sayest thou, 'The Son of man must be lifted up?' Who is this Son of man?"

Then Jesus said unto them, "Yet a little while is the light with you. Walk while ye have the light, lest darkness come upon you, for he that walketh in darkness knoweth not whither he goeth.

"While ye have light, believe in the light, that ye may be the children of light."

John 12:20–36a

YET THEY BELIEVED NOT ON HIM

These things spake Jesus, and [he] departed, and did hide himself from them.

But though he had done so many miracles before them, yet they believed not on him, that the saying of Esaias the prophet might be fulfilled, which he spake, "Lord, who hath believed our report, and to whom hath the arm of the Lord been revealed?"

Therefore they could not believe, because that Esaias said again, "He hath blinded their eyes, and hardened their heart; that they should not see with their eyes, nor understand with their heart, and be converted, and I should heal them."

These things said Esaias, when he saw his glory, and spake of him. Nevertheless among the chief rulers also many believed on him, but because of the Pharisees, they did not confess him, lest they should be put out of the synagogue, for they loved the praise of men more than the praise of God.

John 12:36b–43

I AM COME A LIGHT INTO THE WORLD

Jesus cried and said, "He that believeth on me, believeth not on me, but on him that sent me. And he that seeth me seeth him that sent me.

"I am come a light into the world, that whosoever believeth on me should not abide in darkness. And if any man hear my words, and believe not, I judge him not. For I came not to judge the world, but to save the world.

"He that rejecteth me, and receiveth not my words, hath one

that judgeth him. The word that I have spoken, the same shall judge him in the last day.

"For I have not spoken of myself, but the Father which sent me, he gave me a commandment, what I should say, and what I should speak.

"And I know that his commandment is life everlasting. Whatsoever I speak therefore, even as the Father said unto me, so I speak.

John 12:44–50

THERE SHALL NOT BE LEFT ONE STONE UPON ANOTHER

And Jesus went out, and departed from the temple, and his disciples came to him for to shew him the buildings of the temple, and one of his disciples saith unto him, "Master, see what manner of stones and what buildings are here!"

And as some spake of the temple, how it was adorned with goodly stones and gifts, Jesus answering said unto him, "See ye not all these great buildings? Verily I say unto you, the days will come, in the which there shall not be left here one stone upon another, that shall not be thrown down."

Matt. 24:1–2; Mark 13:1–2; Luke 21:5–6

WHAT SHALL BE THE SIGN OF THY COMING?

And as he sat upon the mount of Olives over against the temple, the disciples Peter and James and John and Andrew asked him privately, saying, "Master, tell us, when shall these things be, and what shall be the sign thy coming, when all these things shall be fulfilled, and of the end of the world?"

And Jesus answering them began to say unto them, "Take heed that no man deceive you. For many shall come in my name, saying, 'I am Christ,' and shall deceive many. Then the time draweth near. Go ye not therefore after them.

"And ye shall hear of wars and rumours of wars. See that ye be not troubled, for all these things must come to pass, but the end is not yet but by and by."

Then said he unto them, "For nation shall rise against nation, and kingdom against kingdom, and there shall be earthquakes in divers places, and there shall be famines and pestilences and troubles, and fearful sights and great signs shall there be from heaven.

"All these are the beginning of sorrows."

Matt. 24:3–8; Mark 13:3–8; Luke 21:7–19

THE GOSPEL MUST FIRST BE PUBLISHED

"But take heed to yourselves, for before all these, they shall lay their hands on you, deliver you up to councils to be afflicted, and persecute you, delivering you up to the synagogues. Ye shall be beaten and cast into prisons, and they shall kill you.

"And ye shall be brought before rulers and kings, and hated of all nations for my name's sake.

"And it shall turn to you for a testimony against them.

"And the gospel must first be published among all nations.

"But when they shall lead you, and deliver you up, settle it therefore in your hearts to take no thought beforehand what ye shall speak, neither do ye premeditate, but whatsoever shall be given you in that hour, that speak ye—for it is not ye that speak, but the Holy Ghost.

"For I will give you a mouth and wisdom, which all your adversaries shall not be able to gainsay nor resist.

"And then shall many be offended, and shall betray one another, the brother shall betray the brother to death, and the father the son, and children shall rise up against their parents, and kinsfolks and friends shall hate one another. And some of you shall they cause to be put to death.

"And many false prophets shall rise, and shall deceive many. And because iniquity shall abound, the love of many shall wax cold.

"But there shall not an hair of your head perish.

"But he that shall endure unto the end, the same shall be saved.

"In your patience possess ye your souls."

Matt. 24:9–13; Mark 13:9–13; Luke 21:12–19

THE ABOMINATION OF DESOLATION

"And when ye therefore shall see Jerusalem compassed with armies, then know that the abomination of desolation thereof is nigh, as spoken of by Daniel the prophet, where it ought not, stand in the holy place (whoso readeth, let him understand).

"Then let them which be in Judaea flee into the mountains. And let him that is on the housetop not go down into the house, neither enter therein, to take any thing out of his house. And let them which are in the midst of it depart out, and let not them that are in the countries enter thereinto.

"Neither let him which is in the field return back again to take his clothes.

"For these be the days of vengeance, that all things which are written may be fulfilled.

"And woe unto them that are with child, and to them that give suck in those days! But pray ye that your flight be not in the winter, neither on the sabbath day.

"For then shall be great tribulation and great distress in the land, and wrath upon this people, such as was not from the beginning of the creation which God created, unto this time, neither shall be.

"And they shall fall by the edge of the sword, and shall be led away captive into all nations, and Jerusalem shall be trodden down of the Gentiles until the times of the Gentiles be fulfilled."

Matt. 24:15–21; Mark 13:14–19; Luke 21:20–24

EXCEPT THOSE DAYS BE SHORTENED

"And except that the Lord had shortened those days, there should no flesh be saved. But for the elect's sake, whom he hath chosen, he hath shortened the days.

"And then if any man shall say unto you, 'Lo, here is Christ,' or, 'Lo, he is there,' believe him not.

"For there shall arise false Christs, and false prophets, and shall shew great signs and wonders, insomuch that, if it were possible, they shall deceive the very elect.

"But take ye heed. Behold, I have foretold you all things. Wherefore if they shall say unto you, 'Behold, he is in the desert,' go not forth. Or 'Behold, he is in the secret chambers,' believe it not.

"For as the lightning cometh out of the east, and shineth even unto the west, so shall also the coming of the Son of man be.

"For wheresoever the carcase is, there will the eagles be gathered together."

Matt. 24:22–28; Mark 13:20–23

AFTER THE TRIBULATION OF THOSE DAYS

"But immediately after the tribulation of those days there shall be signs: the sun shall be darkened, and the moon shall not give her light, and the stars shall fall from heaven, and the powers of the heavens shall be shaken. And upon the earth, distress of nations, with perplexity, and the sea and the waves roaring.

"And then shall appear the sign of the Son of man in heaven. And then shall all the tribes of the earth mourn. They shall see the Son of man coming in the clouds of heaven with power and great glory.

"And then he shall send his angels with a great sound of a trumpet, and they shall gather together his elect from the four winds, from the uttermost part of the earth to the uttermost part of heaven.

"And when these things begin to come to pass, then look up, and lift up your heads for your redemption draweth nigh."

Matt. 24:29–31; Mark 13:24–27; Luke 21:25–28

THIS GENERATION SHALL NOT PASS

"Verily, I say unto you, that this generation shall not pass, till all these things be fulfilled.

"Heaven and earth shall pass away, but my words shall not pass away."

Matt. 24:34–35; Mark 13:30-31; Luke 21:32–33

PARABLE OF THE FIG TREE

"And he spake to them, "Now learn a parable of the fig tree: behold the fig tree, and all the trees, when his branch is yet tender, and they now putteth forth leaves, ye know that summer is now nigh at hand.

"So likewise ye, when ye shall see all these things come to pass, know ye that the kingdom of God is nigh at hand, even at the doors."

Matt. 24:32–33; Mark 13:28–29; Luke 21:29–31

THAT DAY AND HOUR KNOWETH NO MAN

"But of that day and that hour knoweth no man, no, not the angels which are in heaven, neither the Son, but the Father only.

Matt. 24:36; Mark 13:32

SO SHALL ALSO THE COMING OF THE SON OF MAN BE

"But as the days of Noe were, so shall also the coming of the Son of man be.

"For as in the days that were before the flood they were eating and drinking, marrying and giving in marriage, until the day that Noe entered into the ark, and knew not until the flood came, and took them all away. So shall also the coming of the Son of man be.

"Then shall two be in the field: the one shall be taken, and the other left. Two women shall be grinding at the mill: the one shall be taken, and the other left.

"And take heed to yourselves, lest at any time your hearts be overcharged with surfeiting, and drunkenness, and cares of this life, and so that day come upon you unawares.

"For as a snare shall it come on all them that dwell on the face of the whole earth.

"Take ye heed. Watch ye therefore, and pray always, that ye may be accounted worthy to escape all these things that shall come to pass, and to stand before the Son of man, for ye know not when the time is or what hour your Lord doth come."

Matt. 24:37–42; Mark 13:13; Luke 21:34–36

A MAN TAKING A FAR JOURNEY

"For the Son of man is as a man taking a far journey, who left his house, and gave authority to his servants, and to every man his work, and commanded the porter to watch.

"Watch ye, therefore, for ye know not when the master of the house cometh, at even, or at midnight, or at the cockcrowing, or in the morning, lest coming suddenly he find you sleeping.

"And what I say unto you, I say unto all, 'Watch.'

"But know this, that if the goodman of the house had known in what watch the thief would come, he would have watched, and would not have suffered his house to be broken up.

"Therefore be ye also ready, for in such an hour as ye think not, the Son of man cometh."

Matt. 24:43–44; Mark 13:34–37; Luke 12:39–40

WHO THEN IS A FAITHFUL AND A WISE SERVANT?

"Who then is a faithful and wise servant, whom his lord hath made ruler over his household, to give them meat in due season? Blessed is that servant, whom his lord when he cometh shall find so doing.

"Verily I say unto you, that he shall make him ruler over all his goods.

"But and if that evil servant shall say in his heart, 'My lord delayeth his coming,' and shall begin to smite his fellowservants, and to eat and drink with the drunken, the lord of that servant shall come in a day when he looketh not for him, and in an hour that he is not aware of, and shall cut him asunder, and appoint him his portion with the hypocrites. There shall be weeping and gnashing of teeth.

Matthew 24:45–51

FIVE OF THEM WERE WISE, AND FIVE WERE FOOLISH

"Then shall the kingdom of heaven be likened unto ten virgins, which took their lamps, and went forth to meet the bridegroom. And five of them were wise, and five were foolish.

"They that were foolish took their lamps, and took no oil with them. But the wise took oil in their vessels with their lamps.

"While the bridegroom tarried, they all slumbered and slept. And at midnight there was a cry made, 'Behold, the bridegroom cometh. Go ye out to meet him.'

"Then all those virgins arose, and trimmed their lamps. And the foolish said unto the wise, 'Give us of your oil, for our lamps are gone out.'

"But the wise answered, saying, 'Not so, lest there be not enough for us and you. But go ye rather to them that sell, and buy for yourselves.'

"And while they went to buy, the bridegroom came, and they

that were ready went in with him to the marriage. And the door was shut.

"Afterward came also the other virgins, saying, 'Lord, Lord, open to us.' But he answered and said, 'Verily I say unto you, I know you not.'

"Watch therefore, for ye know neither the day nor the hour wherein the Son of man cometh."

Matthew 25:1–13

WELL DONE, THOU GOOD AND FAITHFUL SERVANT

"For the kingdom of heaven is as a man travelling into a far country, who called his own servants, and delivered unto them his goods. And unto one he gave five talents, to another two, and to another one—to every man according to his several ability—and straightway took his journey.

"Then he that had received the five talents went and traded with the same, and made them other five talents. And likewise he that had received two, he also gained other two. But he that had received one went and digged in the earth, and hid his lord's money.

"After a long time the lord of those servants cometh, and reckoneth with them. And so he that had received five talents came and brought other five talents, saying, 'Lord, thou deliveredst unto me five talents. Behold, I have gained beside them five talents more.'

"His lord said unto him, 'Well done, thou good and faithful servant. Thou hast been faithful over a few things, I will make thee ruler over many things. Enter thou into the joy of thy lord.'

"He also that had received two talents came and said, 'Lord, thou deliveredst unto me two talents. Behold, I have gained two other talents beside them.'

"His lord said unto him, 'Well done, good and faithful servant Thou hast been faithful over a few things, I will make thee ruler over many things. Enter thou into the joy of thy lord.'

"Then he which had received the one talent came and said,

'Lord, I knew thee that thou art an hard man, reaping where thou hast not sown, and gathering where thou hast not strawed. And I was afraid, and went and hid thy talent in the earth. Lo, there thou hast that is thine.'

"His lord answered and said unto him, 'Thou wicked and slothful servant, thou knewest that I reap where I sowed not, and gather where I have not strawed. Thou oughtest therefore to have put my money to the exchangers, and then at my coming I should have received mine own with usury.

"'Take therefore the talent from him, and give it unto him which hath ten talents. For unto every one that hath shall be given, and he shall have abundance, but from him that hath not shall be taken away even that which he hath.

"'And cast ye the unprofitable servant into outer darkness. There shall be weeping and gnashing of teeth.'"

Matthew 25:14–30

UNTO THE LEAST OF THESE MY BRETHREN

"When the Son of man shall come in his glory, and all the holy angels with him, then shall he sit upon the throne of his glory. And before him shall be gathered all nations. And he shall separate them one from another, as a shepherd divideth his sheep from the goats. And he shall set the sheep on his right hand, but the goats on the left.

"Then shall the King say unto them on his right hand, 'Come, ye blessed of my Father, inherit the kingdom prepared for you from the foundation of the world.'

"'For I was an hungred, and ye gave me meat. I was thirsty, and ye gave me drink. I was a stranger, and ye took me in. Naked, and ye clothed me. I was sick, and ye visited me. I was in prison, and ye came unto me.'

"Then shall the righteous answer him, saying, 'Lord, when saw we thee an hungred, and fed thee? Or thirsty, and gave thee drink? When saw we thee a stranger, and took thee in? Or naked, and clothed thee? Or when saw we thee sick, or in prison, and came unto thee?'

"And the King shall answer and say unto them, 'Verily I say unto you, inasmuch as ye have done it unto one of the least of these my brethren, ye have done it unto me.'

"Then shall he say also unto them on the left hand, 'Depart from me, ye cursed, into everlasting fire, prepared for the devil and his angels. For I was an hungred, and ye gave me no meat. I was thirsty, and ye gave me no drink. I was a stranger, and ye took me not in. Naked, and ye clothed me not. Sick, and in prison, and ye visited me not.'

"Then shall they also answer him, saying, 'Lord, when saw we thee an hungred, or athirst, or a stranger, or naked, or sick, or in prison, and did not minister unto thee?'

"Then shall he answer them, saying, 'Verily I say unto you, inasmuch as ye did it not to one of the least of these, ye did it not to me.'

"And these shall go away into everlasting punishment, but the righteous into life eternal."

Matthew 25:31–46

NOT ON THE FEAST DAY LEST THERE BE AN UPROAR AMONG THE PEOPLE

And it came to pass, when Jesus had finished all these sayings, he said unto his disciples, "Now, ye know that after two days is the feast of the passover, and of unleavened bread."

And then assembled together the chief priests, and the scribes, and the elders of the people, unto the palace of the high priest, who was called Caiaphas, and consulted that they might take Jesus by craft, and put him to death, for they feared the people. But they said, "Not on the feast day, lest there be an uproar among the people."

Matt. 26:1–5; Mark 14:1–2; Luke 22:1–2

WHAT WILL YE GIVE ME AND I WILL DELIVER HIM UNTO YOU?

Then entered Satan into one Judas surnamed Iscariot, being one of the twelve. And he went his way, and communed with the chief priests and captains, how he might betray him unto them.

And said unto them, "What will ye give me, and I will deliver him unto you?" And when they heard it, they were glad, and covenanted to give him money—thirty pieces of silver.

And from that time, he promised, and sought opportunity how he might conveniently betray him unto them, in the absence of the multitude.

Matt. 26:14–16; Mark 14:10–11; Luke 22:3–6

❧ V ❧

THE FIFTH DAY OF
THE WEEK

Thursday

GO AND PREPARE US THE PASSOVER

Then came the first day of the feast of unleavened bread, when the passover must be killed. And he sent Peter and John, saying, "Go and prepare us the passover, that we may eat." And the disciples came to Jesus, saying unto him, "Where wilt thou that we prepare for thee to eat the passover?"

He saith unto them, "Behold, go into the city, and when ye are entered in, there shall meet you a man bearing a pitcher of water. Follow him into the house where he entereth in. And wheresoever he shall go in, say ye to the goodman of the house, 'The Master saith unto thee, "My time is at hand. I will keep the passover at thy house with my disciples."

"And he will shew you a large upper room, furnished and prepared. There make ready for us."

And the disciples did as Jesus had appointed them, and went forth, and came into the city, and found as he had said unto them. And they made ready the passover.

Matt. 26:17–20; Mark 14:12–16; Luke 22:7–13

WITH DESIRE I HAVE DESIRED TO EAT THIS PASSOVER WITH YOU

And when the hour was come, in the evening, he came and sat down, and the twelve apostles with him.

And he said unto them, "With desire I have desired to eat this passover with you, before I suffer.

"For I say unto you, I will not any more eat thereof, until it be fulfilled in the kingdom of God."

And he took the cup, and gave thanks, and said, "Take this, and divide it among yourselves, for I say unto you, I will not drink of the fruit of the vine, until the kingdom of God shall come."

Matt. 26:20; Mark 14:17; Luke 22:14–18

THERE WAS ALSO A STRIFE AMONG THEM

And there was also a strife among them, which of them should be accounted the greatest. And he said unto them, "The kings of the Gentiles exercise lordship over them, and they that exercise authority upon them are called benefactors. But ye shall not be so. But he that is greatest among you, let him be as the younger, and he that is chief, as he that doth serve.

"For whether is greater, he that sitteth at meat, or he that serveth? Is not he that sitteth at meat? But I am among you as he that serveth.

"Ye are they which have continued with me in my temptations. And I appoint unto you a kingdom, as my Father hath appointed unto me, that ye may eat and drink at my table in my kingdom, and sit on thrones, judging the twelve tribes of Israel."

Luke 22:24–30

FOR I HAVE GIVEN YOU AN EXAMPLE

Now before the feast of the passover, when Jesus knew that his hour was come that he should depart out of this world unto the Father, having loved his own which were in the world, he loved them unto the end.

And supper being ended, the devil having now put into the heart of Judas Iscariot, Simon's son, to betray him, and Jesus knowing that the Father had given all things into his hands, and that he was come from God, and went to God, he riseth from supper, and laid aside his garments; and took a towel, and girded himself.

After that he poureth water into a bason, and began to wash the disciples' feet, and to wipe them with the towel wherewith he was girded. Then cometh he to Simon Peter, and Peter saith unto him, "Lord, dost thou wash my feet?"

Jesus answered and said unto him, "What I do thou knowest not now; but thou shalt know hereafter."

Peter saith unto him, "Thou shalt never wash my feet." Jesus answered him, "If I wash thee not, thou hast no part with me." Simon Peter saith unto him, "Lord, not my feet only, but also my hands and my head."

Jesus saith to him, "He that is washed needeth not save to wash his feet, but is clean every whit. And ye are clean, but not all." For he knew who should betray him; therefore said he, "Ye are not all clean."

So after he had washed their feet, and had taken his garments, and was set down again, he said unto them, "Know ye what I have done to you? Ye call me Master and Lord, and ye say well, for so I am. If I then, your Lord and Master, have washed your feet, ye also ought to wash one another's feet.

"For I have given you an example, that ye should do as I have done to you.

"Verily, verily, I say unto you, the servant is not greater than his lord, neither he that is sent greater than he that sent him. If ye know these things, happy are ye if ye do them.

"I speak not of you all. I know whom I have chosen, but that the scripture may be fulfilled, 'He that eateth bread with me hath lifted up his heel against me.'

"Now I tell you before it come, that, when it is come to pass, ye may believe that I am he. Verily, verily, I say unto you, he that receiveth whomsoever I send receiveth me, and he that receiveth me receiveth him that sent me."

John 13:1–20; Psalms 41:9

ONE OF YOU SHALL BETRAY ME

"I speak not of you all. I know whom I have chosen, but that the scripture may be fulfilled, 'He that eateth bread with me hath lifted up his heel against me.'

"Now I tell you before it come, that, when it is come to pass, ye may believe that I am he."

And when Jesus had thus said, as they sat and did eat, he was troubled in spirit, and testified, and said, "But, behold, verily, verily, I say unto you, that one of you which eateth with me shall betray me. The hand of him that betrayeth me is with me on the table."

Then the disciples looked one on another, doubting of whom he spake. And they began to enquire among themselves, which of them it was that should do this thing. And they began to be exceeding sorrowful, and began every one of them to say unto him, "Lord, is it I?" And another said, "Is it I?"

And he answered and said unto them, "It is one of the twelve, that dippeth his hand with me in the dish, the same shall betray me. And truly the Son of man indeed goeth, as it is written of him. But woe to that man by whom the Son of man is betrayed! Good were it for that man if he had never been born."

Then Judas, which betrayed him, answered and said, "Master, is it I?"

He said unto him, "Thou hast said."

Matt. 26:21–25; Mark 14:18–21; Luke 22:21–23; John 13:21–22

THAT THOU DOEST, DO QUICKLY

Now there was leaning on Jesus' bosom one of his disciples, whom Jesus loved. Simon Peter therefore beckoned to him, that he should ask who it should be of whom he spake. He then lying on Jesus' breast saith unto him, "Lord, who is it?"

Jesus answered, "He it is, to whom I shall give a sop, when I have dipped it." And when he had dipped the sop, he gave it to Judas Iscariot, the son of Simon.

And after the sop, Satan entered into him. Then said Jesus unto him, "That thou doest, do quickly."

Now no man at the table knew for what intent he spake this unto him. For some of them thought, because Judas had the bag, that Jesus had said unto him, "Buy those things that we have need of against the feast," or that he should give something to the poor.

He then having received the sop went immediately out. And it was night.

John 13:23–30

LOVE ONE ANOTHER

Therefore, when he was gone out, Jesus said, "Now is the Son of man glorified, and God is glorified in him. If God be glorified in him, God shall also glorify him in himself, and shall straightway glorify him.

"Little children, yet a little while I am with you. Ye shall seek me, and, as I said unto the Jews, 'Whither I go, ye cannot come,' so now I say to you, A new commandment I give unto you, that ye love one another; as I have loved you, that ye also love one another. By this shall all men know that ye are my disciples, if ye have love one to another."

John 13:31–35

JESUS TOOK BREAD AND BLESSED IT

And as they were eating, Jesus took bread, and blessed it, and gave thanks and brake it, and gave it to the disciples and said, "Take, eat. This is my body which is given for you. This do in remembrance of me."

And he took the cup, and when he had given thanks and he gave it to them, saying, "Drink ye all of it," and they all drank of it.

And he said unto them, "This is my blood of the new testament, which is shed for many for the remission of sins. But verily I say unto you, I will not drink henceforth of this fruit of the vine, until that day when I drink it new with you in my Father's kingdom."

Matt. 26:26–29; Mark 14:22–25; Luke 22:19–20

BEFORE THE COCK CROW TWICE

Then saith Jesus unto them, "All ye shall be offended because of me this night, for it is written, 'I will smite the shepherd, and the sheep of the flock shall be scattered abroad.' But after that I am risen again, I will go before you into Galilee."

But Peter answered and said unto him, "Though all men shall be offended because of thee, yet will I never be offended."

And the Lord said, "Simon, Simon, behold, Satan hath desired to have you, that he may sift you as wheat. But I have prayed for thee, that thy faith fail not. And when thou art converted, strengthen thy brethren."

Simon Peter said unto him, "Lord, whither goest thou?" Jesus answered him, "Whither I go, thou canst not follow me now, but thou shalt follow me afterwards."

And Peter said unto him, "Lord, why cannot I follow thee now? I am ready to go with thee, both into prison, and to death. I will lay down my life for thy sake."

And Jesus answered him, "Wilt thou lay down thy life for my sake? Verily I say unto thee, that this day, even in this night, before the cock crow twice, thou shalt thrice deny that thou knowest me."

But Peter said unto him the more vehemently, "Though I should die with thee, yet will I not deny thee in any wise." Likewise also said all the disciples.

And he said unto them, "When I sent you without purse, and scrip, and shoes, lacked ye any thing?" And they said, "Nothing."

Then said he unto them, "But now, he that hath a purse, let him take it, and likewise his scrip, and he that hath no sword, let him sell his garment, and buy one.

"For I say unto you, that this that is written must yet be accomplished in me, 'And he was reckoned among the transgressors,' for the things concerning me have an end."

And they said, "Lord, behold, here are two swords." And he said unto them, "It is enough."

Matt. 26:31–35; Mark 14:27–31; Luke 22:31–38; John 13:36–38

I AM THE WAY, THE TRUTH, AND THE LIFE

"Let not your heart be troubled. Ye believe in God, believe also in me. In my Father's house are many mansions. If it were not so, I would have told you. I go to prepare a place for you.

"And if I go and prepare a place for you, I will come again, and receive you unto myself, that where I am, there ye may be also. And whither I go ye know, and the way ye know."

Thomas saith unto him, "Lord, we know not whither thou goest, and how can we know the way?"

Jesus saith unto him, "I am the way, the truth, and the life. No man cometh unto the Father, but by me.

"If ye had known me, ye should have known my Father also, and from henceforth ye know him, and have seen him."

Philip saith unto him, "Lord, shew us the Father, and it sufficeth us." Jesus saith unto him, "Have I been so long time with you, and yet hast thou not known me, Philip? He that hath seen me hath seen the Father; and how sayest thou then, 'Shew us the Father'? Believest thou not that I am in the Father, and the Father in me?

The words that I speak unto you I speak not of myself, but the Father that dwelleth in me, he doeth the works.

"Believe me that I am in the Father, and the Father in me, or else believe me for the very works' sake. Verily, verily, I say unto you, he that believeth on me, the works that I do shall he do also, and greater works than these shall he do, because I go unto my Father.

"And whatsoever ye shall ask in my name, that will I do, that the Father may be glorified in the Son. If ye shall ask any thing in my name, I will do it.

"If ye love me, keep my commandments.

"And I will pray the Father, and he shall give you another Comforter, that he may abide with you for ever, even the Spirit of truth, whom the world cannot receive, because it seeth him not, neither knoweth him. But ye know him, for he dwelleth with you, and shall be in you.

"I will not leave you comfortless: I will come to you. Yet a little while, and the world seeth me no more; but ye see me. Because I live, ye shall live also.

"At that day ye shall know that I am in my Father, and ye in me, and I in you. He that hath my commandments, and keepeth them, he it is that loveth me, and he that loveth me shall be loved of my Father, and I will love him, and will manifest myself to him."

Judas saith unto him (not Iscariot), "Lord, how is it that thou wilt manifest thyself unto us, and not unto the world?"

Jesus answered and said unto him, "If a man love me, he will keep my words, and my Father will love him, and we will come unto him, and make our abode with him. He that loveth me not keepeth not my sayings, and the word which ye hear is not mine, but the Father's which sent me.

"These things have I spoken unto you, being yet present with you.

"But the Comforter, which is the Holy Ghost, whom the Father will send in my name, he shall teach you all things, and bring all things to your remembrance, whatsoever I have said unto you.

"Peace I leave with you, my peace I give unto you. Not as the world giveth, give I unto you. Let not your heart be troubled, neither let it be afraid.

"Ye have heard how I said unto you, 'I go away, and come again unto you'. If ye loved me, ye would rejoice, because I said, 'I go unto the Father'—for my Father is greater than I.

"And now I have told you before it come to pass, that, when it is come to pass, ye might believe. Hereafter I will not talk much with you, for the prince of this world cometh, and hath nothing in me.

"But that the world may know that I love the Father; and as the Father gave me commandment, even so I do."

John 14:1–31a

ARISE, LET US GO HENCE

"Arise, let us go hence." And when they had sung an hymn, he went as he was wont, to the mount of Olives, and his disciples also followed him.

Matthew 26:30, Mark 14:26, Luke 22:39, John 14:31b

I AM THE TRUE VINE

"I am the true vine, and my Father is the husbandman. Every branch in me that beareth not fruit he taketh away, and every branch that beareth fruit, he purgeth it, that it may bring forth more fruit.

"Now ye are clean through the word which I have spoken unto you. Abide in me, and I in you. As the branch cannot bear fruit of itself, except it abide in the vine, no more can ye, except ye abide in me.

"I am the vine, ye are the branches. He that abideth in me, and I in him, the same bringeth forth much fruit, for without me ye can do nothing.

"If a man abide not in me, he is cast forth as a branch, and is withered. And men gather them, and cast them into the fire, and they are burned. If ye abide in me, and my words abide in you, ye shall ask what ye will, and it shall be done unto you.

"Herein is my Father glorified, that ye bear much fruit, so shall ye be my disciples.

"As the Father hath loved me, so have I loved you: continue ye in my love.

"If ye keep my commandments, ye shall abide in my love; even as I have kept my Father's commandments, and abide in his love.

"These things have I spoken unto you, that my joy might remain in you, and that your joy might be full.

"This is my commandment, that ye love one another, as I have loved you. Greater love hath no man than this, that a man lay down his life for his friends. Ye are my friends, if ye do whatsoever I command you.

"Henceforth I call you not servants; for the servant knoweth not what his lord doeth, but I have called you friends. For all things that I have heard of my Father I have made known unto you.

"Ye have not chosen me, but I have chosen you, and ordained you, that ye should go and bring forth fruit, and that your fruit should remain, that whatsoever ye shall ask of the Father in my name, he may give it you.

"These things I command you, that ye love one another.

"If the world hate you, ye know that it hated me before it hated you. If ye were of the world, the world would love his own. But because ye are not of the world, but I have chosen you out of the world, therefore the world hateth you.

"Remember the word that I said unto you, 'The servant is not greater than his lord. If they have persecuted me, they will also persecute you. If they have kept my saying, they will keep yours also.

"But all these things will they do unto you for my name's sake, because they know not him that sent me. If I had not come and spoken unto them, they had not had sin: but now they have no cloke for their sin. He that hateth me hateth my Father also.

"If I had not done among them the works which none other man did, they had not had sin, but now have they both seen and hated both me and my Father. But this cometh to pass, that the word might be fulfilled that is written in their law, 'They hated me without a cause.'

"But when the Comforter is come, whom I will send unto you from the Father, even the Spirit of truth, which proceedeth from the Father, he shall testify of me. And ye also shall bear witness, because ye have been with me from the beginning."

John 15:1–27; Psalms 69:4

I HAVE OVERCOME THE WORLD

"These things have I spoken unto you, that ye should not be offended. They shall put you out of the synagogues. Yea, the time cometh, that whosoever killeth you will think that he doeth God service. And these things will they do unto you, because they have not known the Father, nor me.

"But these things have I told you, that when the time shall come, ye may remember that I told you of them. And these things I said not unto you at the beginning, because I was with you. But now I go my way to him that sent me, and none of you asketh me, 'Whither goest thou?'

"But because I have said these things unto you, sorrow hath filled your heart. Nevertheless I tell you the truth; It is expedient for you that I go away, for if I go not away, the Comforter will not come unto you, but if I depart, I will send him unto you.

"And when he is come, he will reprove the world of sin, and of righteousness, and of judgment. Of sin, because they believe not on me. Of righteousness, because I go to my Father, and ye see me no more. Of judgment, because the prince of this world is judged.

"I have yet many things to say unto you, but ye cannot bear them now.

"Howbeit when he, the Spirit of truth, is come, he will guide you into all truth, for he shall not speak of himself. But whatsoever he shall hear, that shall he speak, and he will shew you things to come. He shall glorify me, for he shall receive of mine, and shall shew it unto you.

"All things that the Father hath are mine, therefore, said I, that he shall take of mine, and shall shew it unto you. A little while, and ye shall not see me, and again, a little while, and ye shall see me, because I go to the Father."

Then said some of his disciples among themselves, "What is this that he saith unto us, 'A little while, and ye shall not see me. And again, a little while, and ye shall see me, because I go to the Father?'"

They said therefore, "What is this that he saith, 'A little while?' We cannot tell what he saith."

Now Jesus knew that they were desirous to ask him, and said unto them, "Do ye enquire among yourselves of that I said, 'A little while, and ye shall not see me, and again, a little while, and ye shall see me?'

"Verily, verily, I say unto you, that ye shall weep and lament, but the world shall rejoice. And ye shall be sorrowful, but your sorrow shall be turned into joy. A woman when she is in travail hath sorrow, because her hour is come, but as soon as she is delivered of the child, she remembereth no more the anguish, for joy that a man is born into the world.

"And ye now therefore have sorrow, but I will see you again, and your heart shall rejoice, and your joy no man taketh from you.

"And in that day ye shall ask me nothing. Verily, verily, I say unto you, whatsoever ye shall ask the Father in my name, he will give it you. Hitherto have ye asked nothing in my name. Ask, and ye shall receive, that your joy may be full.

"These things have I spoken unto you in proverbs, but the time cometh, when I shall no more speak unto you in proverbs, but I shall shew you plainly of the Father. At that day ye shall ask in my name, and I say not unto you, that I will pray the Father for you. For the Father himself loveth you, because ye have loved me, and have believed that I came out from God. I came forth from the Father, and am come into the world. Again, I leave the world, and go to the Father."

His disciples said unto him, "Lo, now speakest thou plainly, and speakest no proverb. Now are we sure that thou knowest all things, and needest not that any man should ask thee. By this we believe that thou camest forth from God."

Jesus answered them, "Do ye now believe? Behold, the hour cometh, yea, is now come, that ye shall be scattered, every man to his own, and shall leave me alone, and yet I am not alone, because the Father is with me. These things I have spoken unto you, that in me ye might have peace. In the world ye shall have tribulation, but be of good cheer; I have overcome the world."

John 16:1–33

THAT THEY MAY BE ONE EVEN AS WE ARE ONE

These words spake Jesus, and lifted up his eyes to heaven, and said, "Father, the hour is come. Glorify thy Son, that thy Son also may glorify thee.

"As thou hast given him power over all flesh, that he should give eternal life to as many as thou hast given him. And this is life eternal, that they might know thee the only true God, and Jesus Christ, whom thou hast sent.

"I have glorified thee on the earth. I have finished the work which thou gavest me to do. And now, O Father, glorify thou me with thine own self with the glory which I had with thee before the world was.

"I have manifested thy name unto the men which thou gavest me out of the world. Thine they were, and thou gavest them me, and they have kept thy word. Now they have known that all things whatsoever thou hast given me are of thee.

"For I have given unto them the words which thou gavest me, and they have received them, and have known surely that I came out from thee, and they have believed that thou didst send me.

"I pray for them. I pray not for the world, but for them which thou hast given me, for they are thine. And all mine are thine, and thine are mine, and I am glorified in them.

"And now I am no more in the world, but these are in the world, and I come to thee. Holy Father, keep through thine own name those whom thou hast given me, that they may be one, as we are.

"While I was with them in the world, I kept them in thy name. Those that thou gavest me I have kept, and none of them is lost, but the son of perdition, that the scripture might be fulfilled.

"And now come I to thee, and these things I speak in the world, that they might have my joy fulfilled in themselves.

"I have given them thy word, and the world hath hated them, because they are not of the world, even as I am not of the world.

"I pray not that thou shouldest take them out of the world, but that thou shouldest keep them from the evil. They are not of the world, even as I am not of the world. Sanctify them through thy truth. Thy word is truth.

"As thou hast sent me into the world, even so have I also sent them into the world. And for their sakes I sanctify myself, that they also might be sanctified through the truth.

"Neither pray I for these alone, but for them also which shall believe on me through their word, that they all may be one, as thou, Father, art in me, and I in thee, that they also may be one in us, that the world may believe that thou hast sent me.

"And the glory which thou gavest me, I have given them, that they may be one, even as we are one. I in them, and thou in me, that they may be made perfect in one, and that the world may know that thou hast sent me, and hast loved them, as thou hast loved me.

"Father, I will that they also, whom thou hast given me, be with me where I am, that they may behold my glory, which thou hast given me, for thou lovedst me before the foundation of the world.

"O righteous Father, the world hath not known thee, but I have known thee, and these have known that thou hast sent me. And I have declared unto them thy name, and will declare it, that the love wherewith thou hast loved me may be in them, and I in them."

John 17:1–26

A PLACE CALLED GETHSEMANE

When Jesus had spoken these words, he went forth with his disciples over the brook Cedron unto a place where was a garden which was named Gethsemane, into the which he entered.

And he saith unto the disciples, "Sit ye here, while I shall go and pray yonder."

And when he was at the place, he said unto them, "Pray that ye enter not into temptation." And he taketh with him Peter and James and John, the two sons of Zebedee, and began to be sorrowful, sore amazed, and very heavy.

Then saith he unto them, "My soul is exceeding sorrowful, even unto death. Tarry ye here, and watch with me."

And he went a little further from them, about a stone's cast, and kneeled down, and fell on his face on the ground, and prayed that, if it were possible, the hour might pass from him.

"O my Father, Abba, if thou be willing, all things are possible unto thee. Let this cup pass from me. Nevertheless not my will, but thine, be done."

And there appeared an angel unto him from heaven, strengthening him.

And being in an agony he prayed more earnestly, and his sweat was as it were great drops of blood falling down to the ground.

And when he rose up from prayer, and was come unto the disciples, he found them sleeping for sorrow, and saith unto Peter, "Simon, sleepest thou? What, could ye not watch with me one hour? Watch ye and pray, lest ye enter into temptation. The spirit truly is willing, but the flesh is weak."

And again, he went away the second time, and prayed and spake the same words, saying, "O my Father, if this cup may not pass away from me, except I drink it, thy will be done."

And when he returned and he found them asleep again—for their eyes were heavy, neither wist they what to answer him. And he left them, and went away again, and prayed the third time, saying the same words.

Then he cometh the third time and saith unto them, "Sleep on now, and take your rest. Behold, it is enough, the hour is at hand, and the Son of man is betrayed into the hands of sinners.

"Rise, let us be going—behold, he is at hand that doth betray me."

Matt. 26:36–46; Mark 14:32–42; Luke 22:40–46; John 18:1

VI

THE SIXTH DAY OF
THE WEEK

Friday

❧ 6 ❧

BETRAYEST THOU THE SON OF MAN WITH A KISS?

AND JUDAS ALSO, WHICH BETRAYED HIM, knew the place, for Jesus ofttimes resorted thither with his disciples. And immediately, while he yet spake, lo, he that was called Judas, one of the twelve, cometh thither, and with him a great multitude—a band of men and officers, with swords and staves, lanterns and torches—from the chief priests and the scribes and Pharisees, and the elders of the people.

And Judas drew near unto Jesus to kiss him. Now he that betrayed him had given them a token, saying, "Whomsoever I shall kiss, that same is he. Take him and hold him fast, and lead him away safely."

And as soon as he was come, he goeth straightway to Jesus, and saith, "Hail! Master, master," and kissed him.

But Jesus said unto him, "Judas, friend, wherefore art thou come? Betrayest thou the Son of man with a kiss?"

Matt. 26:47–50; Mark 14:43–45; Luke 22:47–48; John 18:2–3

WHOM SEEK YE?

Jesus therefore, knowing all things that should come upon him, went forth, and said unto them, "Whom seek ye?"

They answered him, "Jesus of Nazareth."

Jesus saith unto them, "I am he." And Judas also, which betrayed him, stood with them.

As soon then as he had said unto them, "I am he," they went backward, and fell to the ground.

Then asked he them again, "Whom seek ye?" And they said, "Jesus of Nazareth."

Jesus answered, "I have told you that I am he. If therefore ye seek me, let these go their way"—that the saying might be fulfilled, which he spake, "Of them which thou gavest me have I lost none."

John 17:12b; 18:4–9

ALL THEY THAT TAKE THE SWORD SHALL PERISH WITH THE SWORD

When they which were about him saw what would follow, they said unto him, "Lord, shall we smite with the sword?"

And, behold, one of them, Simon Peter, which was with Jesus, stretched out his hand, and having a sword drew it, and smote the high priest's servant, and cut off his right ear. The servant's name was Malchus.

And Jesus answered and said, "Suffer ye thus far." And he touched his ear, and healed him.

Then said Jesus unto Peter, "Put up again thy sword into the sheath—for all they that take the sword shall perish with the sword.

"Thinkest thou that I cannot now pray to my Father, and he shall presently give me more than twelve legions of angels? But how then shall the scriptures be fulfilled, that thus it must be?

"The cup which my Father hath given me, shall I not drink it?

And in that same hour Jesus answered and said unto the chief priests, and captains of the temple, and the elders, which were come to him, "Are ye come out as against a thief with swords and with staves for to take me?

"When I was daily with you in the temple, ye stretched forth no hands against me. But this is your hour, and the power of darkness."

Matt. 26:51–55; Mark 14:47–49; Luke 22:49–53; John 18:10–11

ALL THE DISCIPLES FORSOOK HIM

Then came the band and the captain and officers of the Jews and laid their hands on Jesus, and took him and bound him. But all this was done, that the scriptures of the prophets might be fulfilled. Then all the disciples forsook him, and fled.

And there followed him a certain young man, having a linen cloth cast about his naked body. And the young men laid hold on him, and he left the linen cloth, and fled from them naked.

Matt. 26:50b,56; Mark 14:46,50–52; John 18:12

INTO THE HIGH PRIEST'S HOUSE

And then they that had laid hold on Jesus took him, and led him, and brought him away into the high priest's house—to Annas first, for he was father-in-law to Caiaphas, which was the high priest that same year.

And with him were assembled all the chief priests and the elders and the scribes. Now Caiaphas was he, which gave counsel to the Jews, that it was expedient that one man should die for the people.

But Simon Peter followed Jesus afar off and so did another disciple. That disciple was known unto the high priest, and went in with Jesus, even into the palace of the high priest. But Peter stood at the door without.

Then went out that other disciple, which was known unto the high priest, and spake unto her that kept the door, and brought in Peter.

And Peter went in, and sat down among the servants and officers who stood there, to see the end.

When they kindled a fire of coals in the midst of the hall, they were set down together, for it was cold. And they warmed themselves. And Peter stood with them, and warmed himself at the fire.

Matt. 26:57–58; Mark 14:53–54; Luke 22:54–55;
John 11:50b; 18:13–18

ART THOU THE CHRIST, THE SON OF THE BLESSED?

Now the chief priests, and elders, and all the council, sought for false witness against Jesus, to put him to death, but found none. Yea, though many false witnesses came, yet found they none. For many bare false witness against him, but their witness agreed not together.

And at the last there arose two false witnesses, and bare false witness against him, saying, "We heard this fellow say, 'I am able to destroy the temple of God, that is made with hands, and within three days, I will build another made without hands."

But neither so did their witness agree together.

And the high priest stood up in the midst, and asked Jesus, saying, "Answerest thou nothing? What is it which these witness against thee?"

But Jesus held his peace and answered nothing.

And the high priest answered and said unto him, "I adjure thee by the living God, that thou tell us whether thou be the Christ, the Son of the Blessed?"

And Jesus saith unto him, "I am, as thou hast said. Nevertheless I say unto you, hereafter ye shall see the Son of man sitting on the right hand of power, and coming in the clouds of heaven."

Then the high priest rent his clothes, and saith, "He hath spoken blasphemy! What further need have we of any witnesses? Behold, now ye have heard his blasphemy. What think ye?"

And they all condemned him and said, "He is guilty of death."

Matt. 26:59–66; Mark 14:55–64

PROPHESY UNTO US, THOU CHRIST

Then the men that held Jesus mocked him, and some began to spit on him, and when they had blindfolded him, they struck him on the face.

And the servants did strike him with the palms of their hands, and say unto him, "Prophesy unto us, thou Christ. Who is he that smote thee?" And many other things blasphemously spake they against him.

Matt. 26:67–68; Mark 14:65; Luke 22:63–65

THOU ALSO WAST WITH JESUS OF NAZARETH

And as Peter was beneath in the palace, there one of the maids of the high priest that kept the door came unto him. And when she saw Peter as he sat by the fire warming himself, she looked upon him, and said, "Thou also wast with Jesus of Nazareth."

But he denied him before them all, saying, "Woman, I know him not, neither understand I what thou sayest."

And when Simon Peter was gone out into the porch, and stood and warmed himself, the cock crew.

And after a little while another maid saw him again and began to say to them that stood by, "This fellow was also with Jesus of Nazareth." They said therefore unto him, "Art not thou also one of his disciples?"

And again he denied with an oath, and said, "Man, I am not. I do not know the man."

And after a while came unto him they that stood by, and confidently affirmed again to Peter, "Did not I see thee in the garden with him? Surely thou also art one of them, for thou art a Galilaean, and thy speech bewrayeth thee and agreeth thereto."

Then Peter began to curse and to swear, saying, "Man, I know not what thou sayest of this man of whom ye speak."

And immediately, while he yet spake, the second time the cock crew.

And the Lord turned, and looked upon Peter.

And Peter remembered the word of Jesus, how he had said unto him, "Before the cock crow twice, thou shalt deny me thrice."

And when he thought thereon, Peter went out, and wept bitterly.

Matt. 26:69–75; Mark 14:66–72; Luke 22:56–62; John 18:17,25–27

WHEN THE MORNING WAS COME

And as soon as it was day, straightway when the morning was come, all the chief priests and elders of the people and the scribes took counsel against Jesus to put him to death, and led him into their council, saying, "Art thou the Christ? Tell us!"

And he said unto them, "If I tell you, ye will not believe, and if I also ask you, ye will not answer me, nor let me go. Hereafter shall the Son of man sit on the right hand of the power of God."

Then said they all, "Art thou then the Son of God?"

And he said unto them, "Ye say that I am."

And they said, "What need we any further witness? For we ourselves have heard of his own mouth."

Matt. 27:1; Mark 15:1; Luke 22:66–71

I HAVE BETRAYED THE INNOCENT BLOOD

Then Judas, which had betrayed him, when he saw that he was condemned, repented himself, and brought again the thirty pieces of silver to the chief priests and elders, saying, "I have sinned in that I have betrayed the innocent blood."

And they said, "What is that to us? See thou to that."

And he cast down the pieces of silver in the temple, and departed, and went and hanged himself.

And the chief priests took the silver pieces, and said, "It is not lawful for to put them into the treasury, because it is the price of blood."

And they took counsel, and bought with them the potter's field, to bury strangers in. Wherefore that field was called "The field of blood" unto this day.

Then was fulfilled that which was spoken by Jeremy the prophet, saying, "And they took the thirty pieces of silver, the price of him that was valued, whom they of the children of Israel did value. And gave them for the potter's field, as the Lord appointed me."

Matt. 27:3–10; Zech. 11:12–13

WHEN HEROD SAW JESUS

And when Herod saw Jesus, he was exceeding glad, for he was desirous to see him of a long season, because he had heard many things of him, and he hoped to have seen some miracle done by him.

Then he questioned with him in many words, but he answered him nothing. And the chief priests and scribes stood and vehemently accused him.

And Herod with his men of war set him at nought, and mocked him, and arrayed him in a gorgeous robe, and sent him again to Pilate.

And the same day Pilate and Herod were made friends together, for before they were at enmity between themselves.

Luke 23:8–12

LET HIM BE CRUCIFIED!

And Pilate, when he had called together the chief priests and the rulers and the people, said unto them, "Ye have brought this man unto me, as one that perverteth the people. And, behold, I, having examined him before you, have found no fault in this man touching those things whereof ye accuse him—no, nor yet Herod, for I sent you to him—and, lo, nothing worthy of death is done unto him. I will therefore chastise him, and release him."

Now at that feast of the passover, the governor was of necessity wont to release unto the people one prisoner, whomsoever they desired.

And they had then a notable prisoner, called Barabbas, which lay bound with them that had made insurrection with him, and who had committed murder in the insurrection.

And the multitude crying aloud began to desire him to do as he had ever done unto them.

Therefore when they were gathered together, Pilate answered them, saying, "Whom will ye therefore that I release unto you: Barabbas, or Jesus which is called Christ, the King of the Jews? For he knew that for envy the chief priests had delivered him.

When he was set down on the judgment seat, his wife sent unto him, saying, "Have thou nothing to do with that just man, for I have suffered many things this day in a dream because of him."

But the chief priests and elders persuaded the multitude that they should ask Barabbas, and destroy Jesus.

The governor answered and said unto them, "Whether of the twain will ye that I release unto you?" And they cried out all at once, saying, "Away with this man, and release unto us Barabbas." (Now Barabbas was a robber who for a certain sedition made in the city, and for murder, was cast into prison.)

And Pilate, therefore, willing to release Jesus, answered and said again unto them, "What will ye that I shall do then with Jesus which is called Christ, the King of the Jews?"

And they all cried out again saying unto him, "Let him be crucified! Crucify him! crucify him!"

And then Pilate the governor said unto them the third time, "Why, what evil hath he done? I have found no cause of death in him. I will therefore chastise him, and let him go."

But they were instant with loud voices and cried out the more exceedingly, requiring that he might be crucified, saying, "Crucify him! Let him be crucified!"

And the voices of them and of the chief priests prevailed.

Matt. 27:15–23; Mark 15:6–14; Luke 23:13–23; John 18:39–40

INTO THE HALL, CALLED PRAETORIUM

Then Pilate therefore took Jesus, and scourged him. Then the soldiers of the governor took Jesus and led him away into the common hall, called Praetorium. And they call together and gathered unto him the whole band of soldiers.

And they stripped him, and clothed him with a purple robe. And when the soldiers had platted a crown of thorns, they put it upon his head, and a reed in his right hand. And they, bowing their knees before him, worshipped him, and mocked him, and began to salute him, saying, "Hail, King of the Jews!"

And they did spit upon him, and took the reed and smote him, and they smote him on the head with their hands.

Matt. 27:27–30; Mark 15:16–19; John 19:1–3

BEHOLD THE MAN!

Pilate therefore went forth again, and saith unto them, "Behold, I bring him forth to you, that ye may know that I find no fault in him." Then came Jesus forth, wearing the crown of thorns, and the purple robe. And Pilate saith unto them, "Behold the man!"

When the chief priests therefore and officers saw him, they cried out, saying, "Crucify him, crucify him." Pilate saith unto them, "Take ye him, and crucify him, for I find no fault in him."

The Jews answered him, "We have a law, and by our law he ought to die, because he made himself the Son of God."

When Pilate therefore heard that saying, he was the more afraid, and went again into the judgment hall, and saith unto Jesus, "Whence art thou?" But Jesus gave him no answer.

Then saith Pilate unto him, "Speakest thou not unto me? Knowest thou not that I have power to crucify thee, and have power to release thee?"

Jesus answered, "Thou couldest have no power at all against me, except it were given thee from above. Therefore, he that delivered me unto thee hath the greater sin."

And from thenceforth Pilate sought to release him, but the Jews cried out, saying, "If thou let this man go, thou art not Caesar's friend. Whosoever maketh himself a king speaketh against Caesar."

When Pilate therefore heard that saying, he brought Jesus forth, and sat down in the judgment seat in a place that is called the Pavement, but in the Hebrew, Gabbatha.

And it was the preparation of the passover, and about the sixth hour. And he saith unto the Jews, "Behold your King!"

But they cried out, "Away with him, away with him, crucify him." Pilate saith unto them, "Shall I crucify your King?"

The chief priests answered, "We have no king but Caesar."

John 19:4–15

AND PILATE GAVE SENTENCE

When Pilate saw that he could prevail nothing, but that rather a tumult was made, he took water, and washed his hands before the multitude, saying, "I am innocent of the blood of this just person. See ye to it."

Then answered all the people, and said, "His blood be on us, and on our children."

And so Pilate, willing to content the people, gave sentence that it should be as they required. Then he released Barabbas unto them (him that for sedition and murder was cast into prison), whom they desired.

And when he had scourged him, he delivered Jesus therefore unto their will to be crucified.

Matt. 27:24–26; Mark 15:15; Luke 23:24–25; John 19:16a

SIMON OF CYRENE

And after that they had mocked him, they took the purple robe off from him. And they took Jesus, and put his own raiment on him, and led him away to crucify him.

And as they came out and led him away, they laid hold upon a man, Simon of Cyrene by name, who passed by, coming out of the country—the father of Alexander and Rufus.

And on him they laid the cross and compelled him to bear it, that he might bear the cross after Jesus.

Matt. 27:31–32; Mark 15:20–21; Luke 23:26; John 19:16

DAUGHTERS OF JERUSALEM, WEEP NOT FOR ME

And there followed him a great company of people, and of women, which also bewailed and lamented him.

But Jesus turning unto them said, "Daughters of Jerusalem, weep not for me, but weep for yourselves, and for your children. For, behold, the days are coming, in the which they shall say, 'Blessed are the barren, and the wombs that never bare, and the paps which never gave suck.'

"Then shall they begin to say to the mountains, 'Fall on us, and to the hills, cover us.'

"For if they do these things in a green tree, what shall be done in the dry?"

Luke 23:27–31

A PLACE CALLED GOLGOTHA

And when they were come, he bearing his cross went forth unto the place which is called in the Hebrew Golgotha, that is, being interpreted, The place of a skull.

And they gave him to drink vinegar, mingled with gall, and when he had tasted thereof, he would not drink, and received it not.

Matt. 27:33–34; Mark 15:22; Luke 23:33; John 19:17

✴ 7 ✴

THERE THEY CRUCIFIED HIM

And it was the third hour, and there they crucified him.
Then said Jesus, "Father, forgive them; for they know not what they do."

With him were there two thieves crucified, on either side one, the one on his right hand, and the other on his left, and Jesus in the midst.

And the scripture was fulfilled, which saith, "And he was numbered with the transgressors."

Matt. 27:38; Mark 15:25,27–28 Luke 23:33b; John 19:18;
Isaiah 53:12b

THE SUPERSCRIPTION OF HIS ACCUSATION

And Pilate wrote a title, a superscription of his accusation, written and set up over his head on the cross. And it was written in letters of Greek, and Latin, and Hebrew, "THIS IS JESUS OF NAZARETH, THE KING OF THE JEWS."

This title then read many of the Jews: for the place where Jesus was crucified was nigh to the city. Then said the chief priests of the Jews to Pilate, "Write not, 'The King of the Jews,' but that he said, 'I am King of the Jews.'"

Pilate answered, "What I have written, I have written."

Matthew 27:37; Mark 15:26; Luke 23:38; John 19:19–22

THEY PARTED MY GARMENTS AMONG THEM

Then the soldiers, when they had crucified him, parted his garments, and made four parts, to every soldier a part, and also his coat—now the coat was without seam, woven from the top throughout.

And they said therefore among themselves, "Let us not rend it, but cast lots for it, what every man should take," that the scripture might be fulfilled, which was spoken by the prophet, "They parted my garments among them, and upon my vesture did they cast lots."

And sitting down they watched him there. These things therefore the soldiers did.

Matt. 27:35–36; Mark 15:24; Luke 23:34b–34c; John 19:23–24; Psalms 22:17b–18

SAVE THYSELF AND COME DOWN FROM THE CROSS

And the people stood, beholding. And they that passed by railed on him, wagging their heads, and saying, "Ah, thou that destroyest the temple, and buildest it in three days, save thyself. If thou be the Son of God, come down from the cross."

And likewise also the chief priests and the rulers also with them mocked and derided him, with the scribes and elders, and said among themselves, "He saved others, himself he cannot save. If he be Christ, the King of Israel, the chosen of God, let him now come down from the cross, and we will see and believe him.

"He trusted in God. Let him deliver him now, if he will have him, for he said, 'I am the Son of God.'"

And the soldiers also mocked him, coming to him, and offering him vinegar, and saying, "If thou be the king of the Jews, save thyself."

Matt. 27:39-43; Mark 15:29-32; Luke 23:35-37

THOU BE WITH ME IN PARADISE

And one of the malefactors, which were crucified with him, reviled him and cast the same in his teeth, saying, "If thou be the Christ, save thyself and us."

But the other answering rebuked him, saying, "Dost not thou fear God, seeing thou art in the same condemnation? And we indeed justly, for we receive the due reward of our deeds, but this man hath done nothing amiss."

And he said unto Jesus, "Lord, remember me when thou comest into thy kingdom."

And Jesus said unto him, "Verily, I say unto thee, to day shalt thou be with me in paradise."

Matt. 27:44; Mark 15:32b; Luke 23:39–43

BEHOLD THY MOTHER

Now there stood by the cross of Jesus his mother, and his mother's sister, Mary the wife of Cleophas, and Mary Magdalene.

When Jesus therefore saw his mother, and the disciple standing by, whom he loved, he saith unto his mother, "Woman, behold thy son!"

Then saith he to the disciple, "Behold thy mother!" And from that hour that disciple took her unto his own home.

John 19:25–27

THERE WAS DARKNESS

Now from about the sixth hour, there was darkness over all the land until the ninth hour.

Matthew 27:45; Mark 15:33; Luke 23:44

ELI, ELI, LAMA SABACHTHANI

And at about the ninth hour, Jesus cried with a loud voice, saying, "Eli, Eli, lama sabachthani?" that is to say, being interpreted, "My God, my God, why hast thou forsaken me?"

And some of them that stood by there, when they heard that, said, "Behold, this man calleth for Elias."

After this, Jesus knowing that all things were now accomplished, that the scripture might be fulfilled, saith, "I thirst."

Now there was set a vessel full of vinegar, and straightway one of them ran, and took a spunge, and filled it with vinegar, and put it on a reed, and put it to his mouth, and gave him to drink.

The rest said, "Let alone. Let us see whether Elias will come to take him down and save him."

Matt. 27:45–49; Mark 15:33–36; Luke 23:45a; John 19:28–29; Psalms 22:1;69:21

IT IS FINISHED

When Jesus therefore had received the vinegar, he said, "It is finished." And when he had cried again with a loud voice, he said, "Father, into thy hands I commend my spirit."

And having said thus, he gave up the ghost.

Matt. 27:50–51; Mark 15:37–38; Luke 23:45b–46; John 19:30

THE VEIL OF THE TEMPLE WAS RENT

And, behold, the veil of the temple was rent in the midst, in twain, from the top to the bottom. And the earth did quake, and the rocks rent.

Matt. 27:51; Mark 15:38; Luke 23:45b

TRULY THIS MAN WAS THE SON OF GOD

Now when the centurion, which stood over against him, and they that were with him, watching Jesus, saw the earthquake, and those things that were done, that he so cried out and gave up the ghost, feared greatly, and glorified God, saying, "Truly this man was the Son of God."

Matt. 27:54; Mark 15:39; Luke 23:47

WITH A SPEAR PIERCED HIS SIDE

The Jews therefore, because it was the preparation, that the bodies should not remain upon the cross on the sabbath day (for that sabbath day was an high day), besought Pilate that their legs might be broken, and that they might be taken away. Then came the soldiers, and brake the legs of the first, and of the other which was crucified with him.

But when they came to Jesus, and saw that he was dead already, they brake not his legs, but one of the soldiers with a spear pierced his side, and forthwith came there out blood and water. And he that saw it bare record, and his record is true, and he knoweth that he saith true, that ye might believe. For these things were done, that the scripture should be fulfilled, "He keepeth all his bones. Of him shall not one of them be broken." And again another scripture saith, "They shall look upon him whom they have pierced."

John 19:31–37; Psalms 34:20; Zech. 12:10

MANY WOMEN WERE THERE BEHOLDING AFAR OFF

And there were also many women there, and all his acquaintance, who stood afar off, beholding these things.

Among whom was May Magdalene, and Mary the mother of James the less and of Joses, and Salome, and the mother of Zebedee's children.

Who also, when he was in Galilee, followed Jesus, and ministered unto him—and many other women which came up with him unto Jerusalem.

Matt. 27:55–56; Mark 15:40–41; Luke 23:49

THEN TOOK THEY THE BODY OF JESUS

And now when the even was come, because it was the preparation, that is, the day before the sabbath, behold, there came a rich man named Joseph of Arimathaea, a city of the Jews—an honourable counsellor, and he was a good man, and a just who also himself waited for the kingdom of God—and was Jesus' disciple, but secretly for fear of the Jews (the same had not consented to the counsel and deed of them).

This man came, and went in boldly unto Pilate and begged the body of Jesus, that he might take him away.

And Pilate marvelled if he were already dead. And calling unto him the centurion, he asked him whether he had been any while dead. And when he knew it of the centurion, then Pilate gave him leave and commanded the body to be delivered to Joseph.

He came therefore, and took the body of Jesus.

And there came also Nicodemus, which at the first came to Jesus by night, and brought a mixture of myrrh and aloes, about an hundred pound weight.

And when Joseph bought fine linen, and had taken the body of Jesus down, he wrapped it in clean linen cloth, with the spices, as the manner of the Jews is to bury.

Now in the place where he was crucified there was a garden, and laid him in his own new sepulchre, which he had hewn out in the rock, wherein never man before was laid.

And he rolled a great stone to the door of the sepulchre, and departed.

And there laid they Jesus, therefore, because of that was the Jews' preparation day, for the sepulchre was nigh at hand. And the sabbath drew on.

And there was Mary Magdalene, and the other Mary, the mother of Joses also, which came with him from Galilee, who followed after, sitting over against the sepulchre, and beheld where his body was laid.

And Mary Magdalene, and Mary the mother of James, and Salome returned, and prepared sweet spices and ointments, and rested the sabbath day according to the commandment.

Matt. 27:57–61; Mark 15:42–47; Luke 23:50–56; John 19:38–42

❧ VII ❧
THE SEVENTH DAY OF THE WEEK

Saturday

✻ 8 ✻

YE HAVE A WATCH

NOW THE NEXT DAY, that followed the day of the preparation, the chief priests and Pharisees came together unto Pilate, saying, "Sir, we remember that that deceiver said, while he was yet alive, 'After three days I will rise again.'

"Command therefore that the sepulchre be made sure until the third day, lest his disciples come by night, and steal him away, and say unto the people, 'He is risen from the dead,' so the last error shall be worse than the first.

Pilate said unto them, "Ye have a watch. Go your way, make it as sure as ye can."

So they went, and made the sepulchre sure, sealing the stone, and setting a watch.

Matt. 27:62–66

❦ VIII ❦
THE LORD'S DAY

Sunday

❦ 9 ❦

WHO SHALL ROLL US AWAY THE STONE?

And when the sabbath was past, very early in the morning, when it was yet dark, as it began to dawn upon the first day of the week, behold, there was a great earthquake.

For the angel of the Lord descended from heaven, and came and rolled back the stone from the door, and sat upon it. His countenance was like lightening, and his raiment white as snow. And for fear of him the keepers did shake, and became as dead men.

At the rising of the sun came Mary Magdalene and the other Mary, the mother of James, Salome, and Joanna, and certain other women that were with them, bringing the sweet spices which they had bought and prepared that they might come and anoint him.

And as they came to see the sepulchre, they said among themselves, "Who shall roll us away the stone from the door of the sepulchre?" for it was very great

And when they looked, they found that the stone was rolled away from the sepulchre

Then [Mary Magdalene] runneth, and cometh to Simon Peter, and to the other disciple, whom Jesus loved, and saith unto them,

"They have taken away the Lord out of the sepulchre, and we know not where they have laid him."

Matt. 28:1–4; Mark 16:2–4; Luke 24:1–2; John 20:1–2

HE IS NOT HERE

And [the other women], entering into the sepulchre, found not the body of the Lord Jesus. And it came to pass, as they were much perplexed thereabout, they saw two young men—one sitting on the right side and one [who] stood by them—clothed in long, white, shining garments.

And they were affrighted and bowed down their faces to the earth, and the angel answered and said unto the women, "Fear not ye. For I know that ye seek Jesus of Nazareth, which was crucified. Why seek ye the living among the dead? He is not here, for he is risen, as he said. Come, see the place where the Lord lay.

"And go quickly, and tell his disciples that he is risen from the dead. Remember how he spake unto you when he was yet in Galilee, saying, 'The Son of man must be delivered into the hands of sinful men, and be crucified, and the third day rise again.'

"But behold, go your way, and tell Peter and his disciples that he goeth before you into Galilee. There shall ye see him, lo, I have told you."

And they remembered his words.

Matt. 28:50–7; Mark 16:5–7; Luke 24:3–8

THEY WENT OUT QUICKLY

And they departed quickly and fled from the sepulchre, with fear and great joy—they trembled and were amazed, and did run to bring his disciples word. Neither said they any thing to any man, for they were afraid.

And told all these things unto the eleven, and to all the rest. It was Mary Magdalene, and Joanna, and Mary the mother of James, and other women that were with them, which told these things unto the apostles.

And their words seemed to them as idle tales, and they believed them not.

Matt. 28:8; Mark 16:8; Luke 24:9-11

THEY RAN BOTH TOGETHER

Peter therefore went forth, and that other disciple, and came to the sepulchre.

So they ran both together, and the other disciple did outrun Peter, and came first to the sepulchre. And he stooping down, and looking in, saw the linen clothes lying, yet went he not in.

Then cometh Simon Peter following him, and ran unto the sepulchre; and stooping down, he beheld the linen clothes laid by themselves, and the napkin, that was about his head, not lying with the linen clothes, but wrapped together in a place by itself.

Then went in also that other disciple, which came first to the sepulchre, and he saw, and believed.

And then the disciples went away again unto their own home, Peter wondering in himself at that which was come to pass, for as yet they knew not the scripture, that he must rise again from the dead.

Luke 24:12; John 20:3–10

TOUCH ME NOT

Now when Jesus was risen early the first day of the week, he appeared first to Mary Magdalene, out of whom he had cast seven devils. Mary stood without at the sepulchre weeping: and as she wept, she stooped down, and looked into the sepulchre, and seeth two angels in white sitting, the one at the head, and the other at the feet, where the body of Jesus had lain.

And they say unto her, "Woman, why weepest thou?" She saith

unto them, "Because they have taken away my Lord, and I know not where they have laid him." And when she had thus said, she turned herself back, and saw Jesus standing, and knew not that it was Jesus.

Jesus saith unto her, "Woman, why weepest thou? Whom seekest thou?" She, supposing him to be the gardener, saith unto him, "Sir, if thou have borne him hence, tell me where thou hast laid him, and I will take him away." Jesus saith unto her, "Mary." She turned herself, and saith unto him, "Rabboni"—which is to say, "Master."

Jesus saith unto her, "Touch me not, for I am not yet ascended to my Father, but go to my brethren, and say unto them, 'I ascend unto my Father, and your Father; and to my God, and your God.'"

And Mary Magdalene came and told the disciples that she had seen the Lord, as they mourned and wept, and that he had spoken these things unto her. And they, when they had heard that he was alive, and had been seen of her, believed not.

Mark 16:9–11; John 20:11–18

BE NOT AFRAID

And as [the other women] went to tell his disciples, behold, Jesus met them, saying, "All hail." And they came and held him by the feet, and worshipped him.

Then said Jesus unto them, "Be not afraid. Go tell my brethren that they go into Galilee, and there shall they see me."

Matt. 28:9–10

AND THE GRAVES WERE OPENED

And the graves were opened; and many bodies of the saints which slept arose, and came out of the graves after his resurrection, and went into the holy city, and appeared unto many.

Matt. 27:52–53

WE WILL PERSUADE HIM AND SECURE YOU

Now when they were going, behold, some of the watch came into the city, and shewed unto the chief priests all the things that were done.

And when they were assembled with the elders, and had taken counsel, they gave large money unto the soldiers, saying, "Say ye, 'His disciples came by night, and stole him away while we slept.' And if this come to the governor's ears, we will persuade him, and secure you."

So they took the money, and did as they were taught, and this saying is commonly reported among the Jews until this day.

Matt. 28:11–15

A VILLAGE CALLED EMMAUS

And, behold, after that he appeared in another form unto two of them, as they walked, and went that same day into the country, to a village called Emmaus, which was from Jerusalem about threescore furlongs.

And they talked together of all these things which had happened. And it came to pass, that, while they communed together and reasoned, Jesus himself drew near, and went with them.

But their eyes were holden that they should not know him.

And he said unto them, "What manner of communications are these that ye have one to another, as ye walk, and are sad?"

And the one of them, whose name was Cleopas, answering said unto him, "Art thou only a stranger in Jerusalem, and hast not known the things which are come to pass there in these days?"

And he said unto them, "What things?" And they said unto him, "Concerning Jesus of Nazareth, which was a prophet mighty in deed and word before God and all the people, and how the chief priests and our rulers delivered him to be condemned to death, and have crucified him.

"But we trusted that it had been he which should have redeemed

Israel, and beside all this, to day is the third day since these things were done.

"Yea, and certain women also of our company made us astonished, which were early at the sepulchre. And when they found not his body, they came, saying, that they had also seen a vision of angels, which said that he was alive.

"And certain of them which were with us went to the sepulchre, and found it even so as the women had said, but him they saw not."

Then he said unto them, "O fools, and slow of heart to believe all that the prophets have spoken. Ought not Christ to have suffered these things, and to enter into his glory?"

And beginning at Moses and all the prophets, he expounded unto them in all the scriptures the things concerning himself.

And they drew nigh unto the village, whither they went, and he made as though he would have gone further. But they constrained him, saying, "Abide with us, for it is toward evening, and the day is far spent." And he went in to tarry with them.

And it came to pass, as he sat at meat with them, he took bread, and blessed it, and brake, and gave to them. And their eyes were opened, and they knew him, and he vanished out of their sight.

And they said one to another, "Did not our heart burn within us, while he talked with us by the way, and while he opened to us the scriptures?"

And they rose up the same hour, and returned to Jerusalem, and found the eleven gathered together, and them that were with them, saying, "The Lord is risen indeed, and hath appeared to Simon."

And they went and told it unto the residue, what things were done in the way, and how he was known of them in breaking of bread, neither believed they them.

Mark 16:12–13; Luke 24:13–35

THE SAME DAY AT EVENING

Afterward, the same day at evening, as they thus spake, being the first day of the week, when the doors were shut where the disciples were assembled for fear of the Jews, came Jesus himself, and appeared unto the eleven as they sat at meat and stood in the midst of them, and saith unto them, "Peace be unto you."

But they were terrified and affrighted, and supposed that they had seen a spirit. And he said unto them, "Why are ye troubled? And why do thoughts arise in your hearts?

"Behold my hands and my feet, that it is I myself. Handle me, and see, for a spirit hath not flesh and bones, as ye see me have."

And when he had thus spoken, he shewed unto them his hands, and his feet, and his side. Then were the disciples glad, when they saw the Lord.

And while they yet believed not for joy, and wondered, he said unto them, "Have ye here any meat?" And they gave him a piece of a broiled fish, and of an honeycomb. And he took it, and did eat before them.

And he said unto them, "These are the words which I spake unto you, while I was yet with you, that all things must be fulfilled, which were written in the law of Moses, and in the prophets, and in the psalms, concerning me."

Then opened he their understanding, that they might understand the scriptures, and said unto them, "Thus it is written, and thus it behoved Christ to suffer, and to rise from the dead the third day. And ye are witnesses of these things."

And then he upbraided them for their unbelief and hardness of heart, because they believed not them which had seen him after he was risen, and that repentance and remission of sins should be preached in his name among all nations, beginning at Jerusalem.

Then said Jesus to them again, "Peace be unto you: as my Father hath sent me, even so send I you."

And when he had said this, he breathed on them, and saith unto them, "Receive ye the Holy Ghost. Whose soever sins ye remit, they are remitted unto them, and whose soever sins ye retain, they are retained."

Mark 16:14; Luke 24:35–48; John 20:19–23

❧ IX ❧
EIGHT DAYS LATER
Sunday

MY LORD AND MY GOD

B UT THOMAS, ONE OF THE TWELVE, called Didymus, was not with them when Jesus came. The other disciples therefore said unto him, "We have seen the Lord." But he said unto them, "Except I shall see in his hands the print of the nails, and put my finger into the print of the nails, and thrust my hand into his side, I will not believe."

And after eight days again his disciples were within, and Thomas with them. Then came Jesus, the doors being shut, and stood in the midst, and said, "Peace be unto you."

Then saith he to Thomas, "Reach hither thy finger, and behold my hands, and reach hither thy hand, and thrust it into my side— and be not faithless, but believing."

And Thomas answered and said unto him, "My Lord and my God." Jesus saith unto him, "Thomas, because thou hast seen me, thou hast believed. Blessed are they that have not seen, and yet have believed."

John 20:24–29

X

THE FORTY DAY
MINISTRY

❧ 11 ❧

I GO A FISHING

After these things Jesus shewed himself again to the disciples at the sea of Tiberias. And on this wise shewed he himself.

There were together Simon Peter, and Thomas called Didymus, and Nathanael of Cana in Galilee, and the sons of Zebedee, and two other of his disciples.

Simon Peter saith unto them, "I go a fishing." They say unto him, "We also go with thee." They went forth, and entered into a ship immediately, and that night they caught nothing.

But when the morning was now come, Jesus stood on the shore, but the disciples knew not that it was Jesus.

Then Jesus saith unto them, "Children, have ye any meat?" They answered him, "No."

And he said unto them, "Cast the net on the right side of the ship, and ye shall find." They cast therefore, and now they were not able to draw it for the multitude of fishes.

Therefore that disciple whom Jesus loved saith unto Peter, "It is the Lord." Now when Simon Peter heard that it was the Lord, he girt his fisher's coat unto him (for he was naked), and did cast himself into the sea.

And the other disciples came in a little ship (for they were not far from land, but as it were two hundred cubits), dragging the net with fishes.

As soon then as they were come to land, they saw a fire of coals there, and fish laid thereon, and bread.

Jesus saith unto them, "Bring of the fish which ye have now caught."

Simon Peter went up, and drew the net to land full of great fishes, an hundred and fifty and three. And for all there were so many, yet was not the net broken.

Jesus saith unto them, "Come and dine." And none of the disciples durst ask him, "Who art thou?" knowing that it was the Lord.

Jesus then cometh, and taketh bread, and giveth them, and fish likewise. This is now the third time that Jesus shewed himself to his disciples, after that he was risen from the dead.

John 21:1–14

LOVEST THOU ME MORE THAN THESE?

So when they had dined, Jesus saith to Simon Peter, "Simon, son of Jonas, lovest thou me more than these?" He saith unto him, "Yea, Lord. Thou knowest that I love thee." He saith unto him, "Feed my lambs."

He saith to him again the second time, "Simon, son of Jonas, lovest thou me? He saith unto him, "Yea, Lord. Thou knowest that I love thee." He saith unto him, "Feed my sheep."

He saith unto him the third time, "Simon, son of Jonas, lovest thou me?" Peter was grieved because he said unto him the third time, "Lovest thou me?" And he said unto him, "Lord, thou knowest all things. Thou knowest that I love thee." Jesus saith unto him, "Feed my sheep."

John 21:15–17

FOLLOW ME

"Verily, verily, I say unto thee, when thou wast young, thou girdedst thyself, and walkedst whither thou wouldest, but when thou shalt be old, thou shalt stretch forth thy hands, and another shall gird thee, and carry thee whither thou wouldest not."

This spake he, signifying by what death he should glorify God. And when he had spoken this, he saith unto him, "Follow me."

John 21:18–19

WHAT SHALL THIS MAN DO?

Then Peter, turning about, seeth the disciple whom Jesus loved following; which also leaned on his breast at supper, and said, "Lord, which is he that betrayeth thee?"

Peter seeing him saith to Jesus, "Lord, and what shall this man do?"

Jesus saith unto him, "If I will that he tarry till I come, what is that to thee? follow thou me."

Then went this saying abroad among the brethren, that that disciple should not die: yet Jesus said not unto him, "He shall not die," but, "If I will that he tarry till I come, what is that to thee?"

John 21:20–23

GO YE INTO ALL THE WORLD

Then the eleven disciples went away into Galilee, into a mountain where Jesus had appointed them.

And when they saw him, they worshipped him: but some doubted.

And Jesus came and spake unto them, saying, "All power is given unto me in heaven and in earth. Go ye therefore, and teach all nations, and preach the gospel to every creature, baptizing them in the name of the Father, and of the Son, and of the Holy Ghost,

"Teaching them to observe all things whatsoever I have commanded you. He that believeth and is baptized shall be saved, but he that believeth not shall be damned.

"And these signs shall follow them that believe; In my name shall they cast out devils, they shall speak with new tongues. They shall take up serpents, and if they drink any deadly thing, it shall not hurt them they shall lay hands on the sick, and they shall recover.

"And lo, I am with you alway, even unto the end of the world. Amen

Matthew 28:16–20; Mark 16:15–18

THIS IS THE DISCIPLE

This is the disciple which testifieth of these things, and wrote these things: and we know that his testimony is true.

And there are also many other things which Jesus did, the which, if they should be written every one, I suppose that even the world itself could not contain the books that should be written. Amen.

John 21:24–25

THAT YE MIGHT BELIEVE THAT JESUS IS THE CHRIST

And many other signs truly did Jesus in the presence of his disciples, which are not written in this book, but these are written, that ye might believe that Jesus is the Christ, the Son of God, and that believing ye might have life through his name.

This is the disciple which testifieth of these things, and wrote these things, and we know that his testimony is true.

And there are also many other things which Jesus did, the which, if they should be written every one, I suppose that even the world itself could not contain the books that should be written. Amen.

John 20:30–31; John 21:24–25

HE WAS PARTED FROM THEM

The former treatise have I made, O Theophilus [friend of God], of all that Jesus began both to do and teach, until the day in which he was taken up, after that he through the Holy Ghost had given commandments unto the apostles whom he had chosen, to whom also he shewed himself alive after his passion by many infallible proofs, being seen of them forty days, and speaking of the things pertaining to the kingdom of God.

And, being assembled together with them, commanded them that they should not depart from Jerusalem, but wait for the promise of the Father, which, saith he, "Ye have heard of me. For John truly baptized with water; but ye shall be baptized with the Holy Ghost not many days hence.

"And, behold, I send the promise of my Father upon you. But tarry ye in the city of Jerusalem, until ye be endued with power from on high."

And he led them out as far as to Bethany, and when they therefore were come together, they asked of him, saying, "Lord, wilt thou at this time restore again the kingdom to Israel?" And he said unto them, "It is not for you to know the times or the seasons, which the Father hath put in his own power.

"But ye shall receive power, after that the Holy Ghost is come upon you, and ye shall be witnesses unto me both in Jerusalem, and in all Judæa, and in Samaria, and unto the uttermost part of the earth."

And when he had spoken these things, he lifted up his hands, and blessed them, and it came to pass, while he blessed them, they beheld [that] he was taken up. He was parted from them and carried up into heaven, and a cloud received him out of their sight.

And while they looked steadfastly toward heaven as he went up, behold, two men stood by them in white apparel, which also said, "Ye men of Galilee, why stand ye gazing up into heaven? This same Jesus, which is taken up from you into heaven, shall so come in like manner as ye have seen him go into heaven."

And they worshipped him, and then returned they unto

Jerusalem with great joy from the mount called Olivet—which is from Jerusalem a sabbath day's journey.

And when they were come in, they went up into an upper room, where abode both Peter, and James, and John, and Andrew, Philip, and Thomas, Bartholomew, and Matthew, James the son of Alphæus, and Simon Zelotes, and Judas the brother of James.

These all continued with one accord in prayer and supplication, with the women, and Mary the mother of Jesus, and with his brethren, and were continually in the temple, praising and blessing God. Amen.

Luke 24:49–53; Acts 1:1–14

www.ingramcontent.com/pod-product-compliance
Lightning Source LLC
Chambersburg PA
CBHW070521030426
42337CB00016B/2048